— Starting —
Motorboating

Also in the Motorboats Monthly series

Practical Motor Cruising
Dag Pike
ISBN 0 229 11827 5

The first title in the series breaks new ground in that it
avoids the formal approach and instead takes the motor
cruiser owner (both novice and experienced) by the hand
to show them the ropes of *practical* motorboat handling
and management.

Dag Pike explains how planing and displacement boats
behave, how to handle them skilfully in all conditions in
harbour, on rivers and at sea, describes what makes them
tick and advises how to get the best from them.

Fast Boats and Rough Seas
Dag Pike
ISBN 0 229 11840 2

This is a more advanced follow-up to *Practical Motor
Cruising*, and is designed to explain advanced handling
techniques for fast boats. With a very practial emphasis,
Pike covers high speed handling as well as operating
techniques in rough weather, all based on personal
experience.

Throughout, Pike's approach is wholly practical, as one
would expect from such a highly experienced seaman.
Even experienced skippers and crew will welcome this
book and value its sound advice, from preparation
through to emergency procedures.

Marine Inboard Engines: Petrol and Diesel
Loris Goring
ISBN 0 299 11842 9

If you quake at the thought of looking under your engine
hatch, this book is the answer to your problems. *Marine
Inboard Engines* is pitched so that it will neither baffle
the newcomer nor bore the old hand, who is sure to learn
a few new wrinkles from these pages. Goring gives
guidance as to which jobs the amateur can safely
undertake – and those which should be left strictly to the
professional engineer.

— Starting — Motorboating

Emrhys Barrell

in association with

World leaders in power

Adlard Coles *Nautical*
London

Adlard Coles *Nautical*
An imprint of A & C Black (Publishers) Ltd
35 Bedford Row, London WC1R 4JH

First published in Great Britain by
Adlard Coles *Nautical* 1991

Photographs by Emrhys and Linda Barrell
and *Motorboats Monthly*

British Library Cataloguing in Publication Data
Barrell, Emrhys
  Starting motorboating.
  1. Motorboats
  I. Title   II. Volvo Penta
  623.8231

ISBN 0–229–11886–0

Printed and bound in Great Britain by
Hartnolls Ltd, Bodmin, Cornwall

Contents

—— 1 ——
Basic decisions

So you want to get afloat. You've seen it on television, read it in magazines, and now you want to get out on the water. Whether you dream of skimming across sunlit seas to anchor in a quiet cove, or making landfall in a foreign port, or just drifting down the river on a Sunday afternoon, there are certain decisions you need to make. In the following pages we hope to help you make the right ones.

Sail or motor?

You have probably already made up your mind about this, but in case you have not, let's just recap. If you have never been afloat before, a motorboat is easier to understand. A steering wheel to turn left or right, throttle and gears to move ahead or astern – the similarities to driving a car are obvious, and while there is more to it than that, this fact alone encourages more newcomers towards powered craft. With a sailing boat, on the other hand, you have to understand the interaction of wind and sail, rigging and ropes. You also generally have to be more fit and active and have a larger crew.

Then too, with a sailing boat, your journeys are more dependent on weather, wind and tides. Arrival times are unpredictable, and so are the conditions you could meet. In a motorboat, while you have to be aware of the above factors, they affect you far less. You can be more sure of when you will arrive, and thus, more important in this busy age in which most of us have jobs to get back to, when you will return.

On the other hand, a motorboat will be noisier, and it uses fuel to run. Neither of these need be a serious problem – modern engines and boats are quiet and smooth, and fuel costs, when looked at in the overall expense of running a boat, will probably average around 10 to 20 per cent of the annual costs.

First decisions

Some of the basic requirements you should take into account when deciding upon your first boat include your age, experience, fitness, family, friends, the amount of time you want to spend boating, the amount of money you want to spend, and where you live.

Age

Your age and fitness should have an important bearing on the boat you choose. The young, fit and active will happily take to the water in fast runabouts. They worry less about the odd faceful of spray, don't mind getting their feet wet when launching the boat, and can cope with bouncing across the waves at high speeds. However, as you get older you will probably look for a boat that is more stable and more comfortable. A boat of 20 to 30 feet in length will give you more comfort at sea, but in rough conditions or at speed even a vessel of this size can be thrown about, and you will have to go for a 30ft boat or longer before you gain real stability. Having said that, I would caution against going too large or you will have difficulty handling and mooring the boat.

On inland waterways, of course, everything is much more peaceful, and a 25ft boat will be quite stable. Then the only limiting factor is dealing with locks and bridges. On the broad and narrow canals of Britain a degree of fitness is required when scrambling up the banks, and working the locks can be heavy going. Most older people can handle one or two locks, but for longer trips you probably will want to have a crew aboard. The alternative is to choose rivers such as the Norfolk Broads, which have no locks, or the Thames, on which all the locks are manned.

Experience

If you have absolutely no boating experience, in your first seasons you should start with modest-sized boats and stay on inland waterways or in sheltered coastal waters. This will enable you to build up your confidence and experience and that of your crew. We recommend that even for your first trips on rivers you should take along an experienced friend. You should also avoid the mistake of turning your first voyages into major outings – a boat full of people with all their attendant gear and picnics increases the pressure on you and transforms minor snags into major disasters. Take your first steps without a large audience, and spend some time reading books and magazines to gain knowledge before you set off.

If you are starting with a sea-going boat some sort of training is essential. This can take the form of purpose-designed courses that teach you the basics of boat handling and navigation. Increasingly, these are being provided by boat dealers and

Inland waterways are more peaceful than the sea. Rivers such as the Thames will also have lock-keepers to help you.

brokers. Alternatively, you can again bring along a knowledge-able friend. Do not go to sea unprepared – you will not enjoy it, and you may soon become another statistic of lifeboat call outs.

Clubs are a useful way to gain experience. You can often crew on other people's boats before deciding on your own, and cruises in company are a safe way to take your first steps farther afield. Users of the inland waterways have large numbers of well-organized clubs, while most coastal ports have at least one.

Family and friends

Boating is normally a social sport. Apart from a few single-handers, most of us take to the water with family or friends, and they should have a strong influence on the type of boat you buy. Don't go for an offshore craft if your partner is afraid of the sea – too many dreams lie permanently tied up in marinas because the first trip frightened everyone aboard. Do not optimistically assume that your teenage children will always want to be with you to help handle your over-large craft. At the same time, if you are likely to cruise frequently with two couples aboard, choose a boat with two well-separated cabins, as the best-designed craft are rarely sound-proof.

Again, if you are not sure what sort of boating is best suited to your family's needs, join a club to find out before you make your purchase.

How much time do you have?

This might sound an obvious question, but it should influence which boat you buy. If your time is precious and you want to spend as much of it as possible afloat, do not buy an old boat or one in need of a lot of maintenance and repair. That tempting bargain in the classified pages will eat up your spare time before even getting it on the water, and even then its probable breakdowns will cause you enormous frustration. Similarly, large boats will generally need more upkeep than small.

In general, inland-waterways boats make better use of your time. They are less affected by the weather, which mean that trips do not have to be cancelled, and they can be used throughout the year.

If you are retired, however, or have a lot of spare time and want to spend much of it on your boat, then your requirements will change. You will want to choose a boat large enough for long-term living, equipped with many of the comforts that you expect at home. You might want a bath rather than a shower perhaps, mains electricity from a shoreline or generator, and a double cabin that can be left made up during the day without encroaching upon the living-space aboard.

How much money do you want to spend?
Be realistic about how much you can afford, and remember to allow enough to cover the annual running costs. A small, well-maintained boat will be safer, more reliable, and will give you more fun and more hours on the water. Buying second-hand will give you more boat for your money, but remember that repair bills will be higher. Do not buy too big a boat and then find that you can never afford to take it to sea. Detailed figures are given in later chapters, but as a rough guide you can expect to spend between 5 and 10 per cent of the purchase price on annual running expenses.

One way of reducing costs is to share the purchase of the boat. Surprisingly few people do this, but it really can work. Suddenly the repair bills and running costs are halved, and the size of boat you can afford is increased. You have to choose carefully who you join forces with, but this isn't too difficult. In some cases the boat will be large enough for you to do your boating together; otherwise you can set up a rota for weeks and weekends. When you actually analyse the number of times you will go afloat, you'll find there's plenty of scope for joint use. A small runabout can be bought and run by two or three single people quite

A runabout will give you fun on the river or sea.

effectively, while a cruiser can be owned by two couples or families. Make sure that you have similar life-styles in terms of how much time you are prepared to put aside for maintenance work, and agree in advance how much you can each afford for boatyard bills and repairs.

Another way of reducing costs is to charter your boat, either to strangers or friends, but this can produce problems of its own as you must decide how much to charge and who should pay for breakdowns or repairs while the boat is in use. We would recommend you think carefully before going down this route.

Where do you live?

The closer your boat is to home, the more you are likely to use it. Having to travel for more than two hours to reach the mooring will seriously reduce your pleasure – after all, you bought a boat to get away from the rat race, not to spend four hours stuck in traffic jams fighting the M3 on a Friday night. However, you do have to assess how hospitable the cruising areas near your home are. If your local coastline is exposed, with few convenient harbours, you will find that much of your time is spent unable to leave the berth. In this case, keeping your boat in a more distant location which has good cruising waters may be a better option. In all cases you have to consider how you want to use your available time, but always remember that boating is meant to recharge your batteries at the end of the week, not drain them.

Hiring and chartering

Up till now we have assumed that you will be buying your boat. However, many opportunities exist for hiring or chartering, and these can be a sensible alternative. If you have never been boating before, hiring allows you to get a feel for what is involved without the outlay of a purchase. On most inland waterways no prior experience is required, and there is no better way of finding out if a waterborne life is really for you. At the same time you will be learning the ropes in someone else's boat – and probably one better designed to take the knocks and bumps of the first-time driver. If you are thinking of buying later, you have the opportunity to look at other craft that you meet underway or tied up to see which might best suit your needs – most boat owners are only too happy to show off their pride and joy and will give you some useful hints, though usually with a bias to their own craft!

To take a boat out to sea on your own you will have to show

some experience, but there are also vessels of varying sizes available with skippers aboard, and again these boats can be valuable in helping you decide whether this is the route to follow. Some people do nothing but hire boats, finding it cheaper and less complicated than buying their own and giving them the option of a new cruising ground every year, both at home and abroad.

Basic types of boat

In the following chapters we will look in detail at the different types of boat available, but here follows a brief run-down of what you can buy and where you can use it.

The two basic boating areas are inland waterways – canals, rivers and lakes – and the sea. The latter can be divided into estuaries, coastal waters and offshore. Most craft are designed for either inland waters or the sea, but while some boats are suitable for both, they generally do not operate as well as purpose-designed models. As we have already mentioned, inland waterways, with their lack of tides, moderate or no currents and few waves, are ideal for your first time afloat. The sea requires more respect, more knowledge and greater experience.

Just as rivers and canals are less demanding on the crew, so they require correspondingly less sophisticated and less expensive boats. The typical river cruiser has a top speed of 7 to 10mph and normally only a single, low-powered engine. On canals speeds are even lower, with a maximum limit of 4mph. Boats can either be cruisers with cabins and berths or dayboats.

For sea-going use you need a stronger, sturdier craft, able to take waves and travel at greater speeds. Twin-engine installations are more common, giving security if one engine should break down.

Finally, there are the fast, open runabouts and inflatables. Usually powered by outboard motors, these boats are light enough to be towed behind a car on a trailer and can therefore be kept at home. They are generally only dayboats, but they still provide the first experience of boating for many people.

Construction materials

In the past, boats were always made of wood, either solid timber or plywood. Light and strong, a wooden boat required skilled men for its manufacture and regular maintenance to prevent it from rotting in the water. During the 1960s wood was gradually replaced by glass-fibre reinforced plastic (GRP), and now nearly all production craft are built this way. GRP consists of layers of glass-fibre cloth, bonded together with a polyester resin to make a hard shell. GRP boats require less skilled labour to build and were thought to be totally resistant to water. Lately it has been shown that they can suffer from a form of surface blistering known as osmosis, but this can be cured, and GRP boats are still much superior to wood in water resistance.

Steel is among other construction materials you may encounter. It is popular with canal boats built in the UK and some river boats, as it is extremely tough and can withstand frequent encounters with lock walls and banks. Dutch companies favour steel construction and use it for both sea-going and river boats. Correctly painted and protected steel will resist the marine environment, but it does need regular maintenance.

Aluminium is also used sometimes for high-speed craft, where its light weight is an asset. It is expensive and requires sophisticated welding techniques, but when correctly looked after it is extremely corrosion resistant.

Other exotic materials include Kevlar and carbon fibre, often bonded with expoxy resins to provide lightweight high-strength hulls, while wood is making a come-back in sophisticated composite materials. These are unlikely to be on your shopping list.

Nautical terms

To help you understand the brochures and the salesman's talk, you need to know the basic parts of the boat and understand some nautical terms. At first some of these expressions might

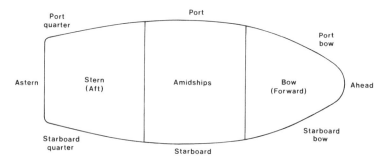

Principal positions and areas on the boat.

sound complicated and unnecessary, but as you become more involved in the sport you will find them increasingly helpful, as they describe things for which there are no equivalent terms ashore.

Port and starboard The left and right sides of the boat. They also describe direction: 'I am turning to port' meaning 'I am turning the boat to the left'.
Forward and aft The front and rear halves of the boat: 'the forward cabin', 'the aft cabin'.
Bow and stern The farthest areas of the boat forward and aft. The bow is also sometimes referred to as the stem, but this is specifically the vertical or near vertical part of the hull. Similarly, the transom is the flat aft surface of the hull.
Midships or amidships The centre of the boat, either in the fore-and-aft sense, or side-to-side.
Ahead and astern These describe direction of movement: 'the boat was moving ahead', 'the boat was moving astern'. They also describe positions of objects relative to the boat: 'we could see the lock ahead', 'the other boat was astern'.
Abeam The position of objects on either side of the boat.
LOA Length overall. The total length of the boat inlcuding the bathing platform and the anchor platform.
Hull length The length of the hull only, excluding platforms or projections.
Waterline length The length of the hull at the waterline.
Beam Overall width at the widest part.
Draught (sometimes spelt draft) The maximum underwater depth of the boat.
Air draught The vertical distance from the waterline to the

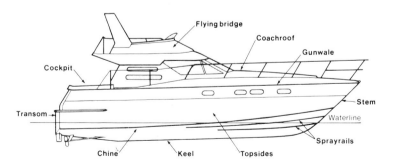

Parts of a typical planing flying-bridge cruiser.

highest point of the boat, used to estimate which bridges it can pass under.

Keel The lowest part of the bottom of the boat. Either the vee shape where the bottom sections meet, or an extension below this.

Spray rails Small corners or steps, running along the bottom of the boat, used to deflect spray downwards and give grip when turning.

Topsides The sides of the hull.

Chine The corner between the bottom and the topsides.

Gunwale The corner between the deck and the topsides.

Coachroof The deck area over the forward cabin.

Cockpit An open-air part of the boat, protected by a raised coaming. Either located aft or amidships.

Flying bridge or fly bridge A raised open area, built on top of the wheelhouse, with seats for passengers and a steering position.

Displacement The weight of the boat. Measured in pounds and tons, or kilograms and tonnes. 1 ton = 2240lb. 1 tonne = 1000kg. 1 tonne = 1.016 tons. Thames Tonnage was an old system based on the length, breadth and draught of a boat. It is no longer used.

Engines

Most boats are powered either by inboard engines, outboard motors, or stern drives. These can be petrol or diesel, or occasionally electric or steam.

Inboard engines, as their name implies, are mounted completely inside the boat and drive a propeller using a shaft. The engines can be either petrol or diesel, and are often but not always based on derivatives of road-going units. Inland boats, use engines of 20–50hp while sea-going craft employ 200–300hp or more.

Outboard motors are clamped onto the transom. They are usually two-stroke petrol units, made from aluminium for lightness. Engine power can range from 2hp for dinghies, through 10–30hp for inland boats, up to 300hp for sea-going craft.

Stern drives, also known as outdrives, Z-drives or inboard-outboards (i/o), are a combination of inboard engine, either petrol or diesel, and a stern-drive unit that can tilt up bolted through the

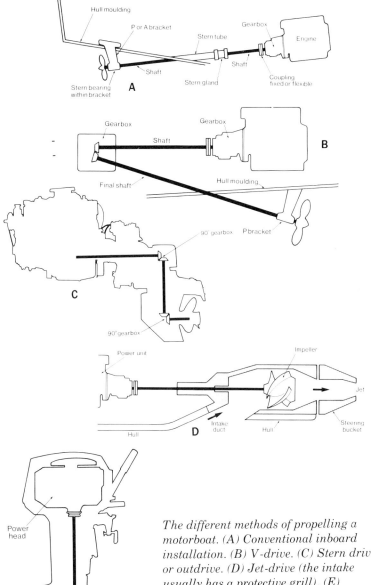

The different methods of propelling a motorboat. (A) Conventional inboard installation. (B) V-drive. (C) Stern drive or outdrive. (D) Jet-drive (the intake usually has a protective grill). (E) Outboard motor.

transom. The advantages of stern drives are accessibility to the propeller and ease of installation. Engine power ranges from 50hp for river use up to 300hp or more in sea-going boats.

V-drives use a system that allows the engine to be mounted aft, with a shaft driving forward from one gearbox into a second gearbox and then back aft through the final shaft. They are not very common but do allow more space in the accommodation area as the engine is mounted under the cockpit.

Jet drives use an inboard engine that drives a large water pump or jet. This sucks water from under the boat, pushing it out aft in a high-speed stream that propels the boat. The advantages are that there are no propeller or underwater fittings to be damaged, allowing the boat to travel in very shallow water. There is also no propeller to injure people in the water, making it popular for the new fun boats.

Electric motors An increasing number of inland boats are using electric motors, run from batteries, to give silent propulsion. These can be mounted either inboard or outboard.

Steam engines Somewhat a specialist rarity used on traditional river launches, these engines are always inboards.

Different engine types

The modern marine engine is an extremely reliable and efficient piece of equipment. Provided it is installed correctly – and equally important is serviced and maintained properly – you should enjoy trouble-free boating. However, there are differences between petrol engines and diesel, inboards and outboards, with each having benefits for some boats and drawbacks in certain applications. In the following paragraphs we look at the different types available and their pros and cons.

Petrol engines

As we have said, petrol engines are invariably marine versions of automotive units. They are lighter, cheaper and easier to service and maintain than diesels. They are also less noisy and vibrate less when running. Their ignition system is electrical, which may corrode and break down in the damp environment of a boat. Their fuel is more expensive, being the same price or more than petrol used on the roads, and they will use 20 to 25 per cent more gallons per hour than a diesel. The fuel is also more dangerous. Petrol, or more specifically its fumes, can be explosive. In a car this is rarely a problem, since any leaks disperse into the air. In a boat with a totally enclosed engine space, fumes can build up. For this reason the engine and fuel installation must be of the highest quality, and preferably fitted with spark-proof extractor fans. Having said all this, instances of fire or explosions on boats are rare and are more often caused by the bottled-gas system used for cooking and heating.

Diesel engines

These are either based on automotive units or are purpose-designed marine models. They are heavier and more expensive to buy. Their fuel system, with its injectors and pump, is more reliable and free from the electrical faults of its petrol rival, but it can be expensive to maintain and repair. A diesel will make more noise and vibration, requiring better sound-proofing of the engine compartment. Fuel is not only cheaper, being tax-free in the UK and around 60p to £1.20 per gallon, but it also does not give off explosive vapours. This is not to say it will not burn if it gets hot enough, but it will not explode. On the down side, the smell, of diesel fuel lingers if you get a leak, so you should ensure that all the tanks, filters and lines are of the highest standard.

Outboard motors

These are the third alternative internal-combustion power source. As its name implies, the outboard motor is clamped onto the transom of the boat, and it is completely self-contained with engine, drive, gearbox and propeller in one unit. Fuel is usually petrol, and in most cases the motor is a two-stroke, with the lubricating oil mixed in the petrol. As a result of this it has nearly double the fuel consumption of a four-stroke petrol or a diesel engine. The advantages are that it is lightweight, easy to install and it can be removed for servicing, storage or repair. Four-stroke models are also available, up to 15hp, with one or two diesel versions up to 25hp.

From the above you can see that the petrol or diesel engine decision is not an easy one. For the smallest boats, up to 20ft on the river or 30ft on canals, the outboard motor is popular, as the overall fuel consumption is not a significant part of the running cost and the other benefits outweigh it. From 18–24ft inboard petrol engines take over, with their advantages for a small craft of quietness and absence of vibration. Above this size, diesel engines move in. The proportion contributed by the engine to the overall cost of the boat is lower, so the higher-priced diesel unit makes less impact. The longer life and lower fuel consumption become significant factors, and the extra reliability of a diesel engine on a bigger boat that will be more at risk from engine failure becomes more important.

The final decision on the propulsion front is whether you opt for an inboard or stern drive installation. We have already briefly described the two systems, but here we give more detail. The inboard engine is usually mounted amidships and drives a propeller that is mounted under the boat through a straight shaft. Where the shaft passes through the bottom of the hull a seal keeps the water out. Steering is achieved by a rudder set behind the propeller. The advantages are a simple and robust installation with few maintenance costs. The disadvantage is that if you should get a piece of rope, plastic bag or weed round the propeller it can be difficult to clear it. The solution is what is known as a weed hatch: a watertight hatch set in a trunk above the propeller. Releasing the hatch allows you to get a hand or hacksaw blade to the propeller to clear it.

The Volvo Penta Duoprop outdrive, fitted here to a V8 petrol engine.

The alternative drive system is the stern drive or out drive. Here the engine is mounted against the transom, driving through it, then down via a Z-drive to the propeller. Its advantages are that it is easier to get to the propeller, and it is simpler for the boat builder to install. The disadvantages are that the underwater unit and its associated gears are vulnerable to damage and can corrode or wear over the years, often requiring costly repairs. Also, since steering is achieved by moving the out-drive unit from left to right, when the engine is in neutral there is very little steerage effect. This is offset by the fact that getting in and out of tight moorings, is considerably easier.

The latest development in stern drives is the Volvo Penta Duoprop. This uses the same outdrive leg, but has a redesigned lower unit that allows two propellers to be fitted, one in front of the other, turning in opposite directions. These contra-rotating propellers give better all round performance than a single prop, with improved acceleration, top speed and fuel consumption. They also improve handling and steering at low speeds with single-engine installations.

2

Inland-waterways cruisers

The inland waterways of Britain and Europe are popular cruising grounds for thousands of motorboats. The River Thames, for instance, has 18,000 licensed craft, of which over 10,000 are private motorboats, the remainder being hire craft and unpowered boats. Other rivers in England and Wales include the Severn and Avon in the west, Trent and Ouse in the north, and the East Anglian waterways of the Great Ouse, the Nene, the Cam, and the Norfolk Broads.

To these must be added over a thousand miles of navigable man-made canals, covering the whole of the country. Built during the latter parts of the eighteenth century and the early years of the nineteenth, the British canal system heralded the start of the Industrial Revolution. The canals joined the major centres of industry and population and carried both raw materials and finished goods. In an age when roads were little more than cart tracks, they reigned supreme for the carriage of every type of product, and at one time canals covered almost 3,000 miles. The coming of the railways heralded their end, and by the middle of the twentieth century freight traffic had almost vanished, with the system falling into disrepair. Gradually, however, their value for leisure use began to be recognized, and now this is virtually their sole purpose.

The canals were built according to either of two sets of dimensions which determined the size of the barges that could use them. The 'narrow' canals had locks that were 70ft long by 7ft wide, while the 'broad' waterways were double this width, and took barges that were the same length but up to 14ft beam. These dimensions have not changed in modern times and still govern the size of boats that can use each part of the system.

The rivers have their own limiting dimensions, based on lock sizes and bridge heights, but in the main the boats they can take are larger than those on the canals. Nearly all parts of the system are interconnected, but if you want to travel on all of it you must have a boat with a narrow beam.

Canals are still waters, with no currents and maximum depths of around 2ft 3in. Built in the days when the horse was the sole means of propulsion they were not designed for high speeds, and even with today's limit of 4mph banks can erode. They are therefore waterways for quiet progress and contemplation of nature. The locks are operated by hand, and the winding gear has changed little over the centuries. Locks can be hard work, sometimes coming in flights of up to twenty or more at a time, but to most crews they rapidly become part of the fun of the trip. Whether providing time to chat with other boat crews as you wait for the chamber to fill, or challenging your team to get the boat through as neatly and swiftly as possible, locks contribute to the satisfaction of the trip.

Of course the system has countless strategically located pubs in which to swap your stories and rest your feet at the end of the day. After all, the bargees of two hundred years ago were as

Locks are part of the fun of river cruising. A busy scene at Goring-on-Thames.

thirsty as you. Here you will find twentieth-century commuter-man discussing animatedly the triumph of covering a distance in a day that he will do in half an hour in his car.

Unlike the canals, rivers are broader, usually deeper and will have some degree of current. They may also have locks, as on the Trent and Thames, or flow freely, such as the placid Norfolk Broads. Bridge heights will generally be greater and boats wider and more powerful. Maximum speed limits will be around 7mph, though even this will be reduced in restricted areas and past moorings. In their lower reaches the rivers become tidal as they meet the sea, and here you can encounter strong currents and streams. Even in their upper reaches in times of rain and flood rivers can run fast, requiring more care in navigation.

Locks, if they occur, will generally be at longer intervals, and often will either be operated by a keeper, as on the Thames, or be easier to work than those on the canals. Since the chamber will usually be larger and able to take more than one boat at a time, the effort of opening the sluices and gates will be shared amongst the crews, and the delays become shorter. For this reason the rivers are more popular, so much so that they can become congested at peak summer weekends, but this is rarely a serious problem.

Boat types

Canal cruisers

As we have already mentioned, the limiting dimensions for boats on the narrow canals are a beam of 6ft 10in, and a maximum length of 70ft. To this must be added a maximum height above the water of around 5ft 6in and a realistic maximum draught of 2ft 3in. Within these limits a specialist craft has developed: the canal narrowboat.

Narrowboats come in all lengths and materials, but the most popular are built in steel and are usually around 40–55ft long. Because their speeds are so low the underwater sections can be nearly square, and the resulting box shape of the craft allows a remarkable amount of accommodation to be built in. A typical 45ft boat will have a saloon forward that converts to a double cabin at night; a galley amidships that will normally be equipped with a domestic-size gas cooker, fridge, and running hot and cold water; a bathroom with shower, sink and WC; and an aft cabin that can have a double berth, two singles, or four bunks.

Thus you can have comfortable accommodation for four to six

people, with all the mod cons of home. Most craft will have some form of central heating to all cabins, and some will even sport microwave ovens, televisions and stereo systems. Headroom inside will be at least six feet throughout. Power comes from a single diesel engine of around 20–40hp, and this will sip fuel at a frugal ⅓–⅔ gallons per hour. As diesel fuel for marine use does not have the same duty as road-going fuel, it will cost you only around 70–90p per gallon at 1990 prices. The steel construction will be usually ¼–⅜in thick, and therefore strong enough to take the knocks of frequent locking.

The price for a new 45ft boat will be between £18,000 and £40,000 at the time of writing, depending on the degree of luxury and finish and the standard of equipment. Second-hand boats can be bought for around £10,000 to £20,000 depending on age and condition.

Narrowboats can be built up to 70ft long, with correspondingly more accommodation, and still fit in the locks, but boats longer than 55ft start to become a handful to control. Two people can easily manage a 45ft boat, but generally with larger boats you will wish you had more crew. The bigger the boat, the harder it is

The author's 45ft narrowboat wends its way through the Welsh countryside on the Llangollen Canal.

to steer around tight bends, and the more vulnerable it becomes to side winds. Smaller narrowboats are also built, with a 30 footer giving comfortable accommodation for two people, but below this size they are usually made from glass fibre.

Glass-fibre canal boats are usually called cruisers to differentiate them from their steel counterparts. Again available with 6ft 10in beam, they are produced from 16 to 32ft. They are lighter in construction than steel boats, allowing them to be powered by outboard motors. Also GRP in theory requires less maintenance, as it does not rust, though this is probably offset by the fact that it is less resistant to continuous knocks and abrasion. In their smaller sizes, up to around 18ft, they are light enough to trail behind a car, thus reducing mooring costs and allowing you to carry out maintenance at home.

The design of glass fibre cruisers usually incorporate a cockpit with seats and a canopy that can be raised in wet or cold weather, making them more comfortable to drive on such occasions. By contrast, the narrowboat skipper braves the elements in the same fashion as the bargees of old. A 16ft two-berth cruiser will cost around £6,000 to £8,000 new, with a four-berth 26 footer around £12,000 to £15,000. Second-hand models can be found from 50 per cent of these prices upwards.

River cruisers

Out on the river the boats can have wider beams, so to achieve a given amount of accommodation they can be shorter overall. Extra clearance under the bridges allows the craft to be taller, further increasing the amount of space down below, while at the same time deck area will be greater. The higher top speeds and likelihood of meeting currents means that engines will generally be more powerful too.

River cruisers are more likely to be constructed of glass fibre, though steel is still used sometimes, particularly in boats that originated in Holland, where steel is popular. Occasionally you will encounter traditional craft made from wood, either solid timber or plywood, and recognizable by their varnished upperworks.

Sea-going boats will also start to make an appearance on rivers, and are recognizable by their overall more powerful look. Tall topsides, flared bows to shoulder aside the waves, flying bridges, often twin engines, and navigational equipment such as radar and VHF aerials all identify these craft.

We'll take a look here at some of the most popular river cruisers, both new and second-hand. In this context it is worth noting that there is no stigma attached to buying a second-hand boat. Many people never own a new boat in their lives, in the same way that most of us never own a new house. Unlike motor cars, boats do not deteriorate rapidly, and in fact many of them improve with age, gaining extra equipment and having all their bugs and teething troubles worked out.

One of the all-time favourites on the river is the Freeman 22 or 23. First launched in 1959 these continued in production until 1975. The layout consists of a main saloon with a four-seater dinette and table that converts to a double berth at night. Forward of this is a small cabin with two single vee berths that can convert to a double. The galley consists of a sink, two-burner cooker with grill, and pressurised cold water. Some models may have had installed an oven, fridge, and instantaneous hot water over the years. A small toilet compartment forward contains a chemical toilet with a self-contained holding tank that you empty out at disposal stations along the river. Lighting is provided by 12V fittings, powered from a battery that is charged by the engine. Out in the cockpit will be a seat to port for the helmsman, with one opposite for the navigator, and a cushioned bench seat across the transom that will take two or three passengers. A canvas cover lifts up on an arrangement like a

*The Freeman 23. A popular first-time four-ber*ʰ river boat.*

pram hood, with plastic windows in the sides, giving protection from the wind and rain.

Power normally comes from a single petrol engine, though a few twin installations and diesel options were built. The engine is usually a marine version of the Ford 1200 or 1500cc car units, though earlier models had the 1172cc side-valve unit. Power is therefore around 30–50hp – more than adequate for the boat and giving a top speed of around 8mph, or 6mph cruising. A Watermota gearbox provides ahead, neutral and astern, plus a reduction ratio to step the engine revs down to to a more suitable speed for the propeller, usually 1.5:1 or 2:1. The drive is taken through a shaft to a propeller mounted under the boat, and steering is via a rudder and car-type wheel.

The Freeman is made of glass fibre, and older boats may suffer from osmosis under the water and from fading of the shiny gel-coat above the water. Underwater treatment, if it has been done, will consist of brushing or spraying on several coats of polyurethane or epoxy paint. Above the water the gloss may have been renewed by a spray application of polyurethane paint to make the boat look as good as new.

Depending on age, condition and model, a Freeman 22 MKI or II, or a Freeman 23 will sell today for £3,000 to £8,000. It will give you a lot of fun and is an excellent way to gain your first experiences on the river. It is small enough to be easy to handle, yet it has enough room for four people. Maintenance costs will be low, with engine servicing simple, and there are few systems to go wrong.

Moving up in size, a 27ft boat will give you more space in both cabin and cockpit. The toilet compartment will normally have a shower, with hot and cold running water as standard. The galley will have an oven, and the boat may well have central heating, either gas or diesel powered. Single engines are still the norm for river use only, but a 27ft craft can tackle short estuary trips, where twin engines will give more security. Petrol engines still appear, but diesels are now more common. Freeman also made a 27, as did several other companies including Seamaster, Elysian and RLM. Prices second-hand can vary between £8,000 and £18,000, with new models also available from other companies at around £20,000.

By 30–33ft you are moving up to craft that will often have a separate aft cabin, with the steering position either amidships in a centre cockpit or outside. The aft cabin gives increased privacy, important on a small boat, plus of course two extra berths. Accommodation will become generally more spacious and comfortable, with facilities nearer to those you expect at home. The Broom 30 typifies this type of craft, providing comfortable accommodation for up to six people. Power comes from a pair of diesel engines, making the boat suitable for short coastal trips yet still handy enough to give you an easy time on the river. The Broom 30 model is no longer in production, but second-hand versions will cost between £25,000 and £35,000. Its modern counterpart, the Broom 10/70, which is 33ft of the most elegant boat you could want, costs from £85,000 upwards. Other boats in this category include the Birchwood 31, Fairline Mirage Aft Cabin, Carver 28 Riviera, Nimbus 26 and 30, and many others.

Above 35ft, privately owned river cruisers tend to be sea-going craft that are being used on the river temporarily or permanently. Bigger purpose-built river boats do exist, but in the main they are hire craft, in which large numbers of berths become important. Included in this category are the 'Bermuda' style cruisers. These originated on the Norfolk Broads, and are recognizable by their flat 'soap-dish' shape, enormous beam, and steering position at the front of the craft. They have masses of space inside, all on one level, with no need to step up and down

The Birchwood 31 has six berths and a separate aft cabin, and is suitable for river or sea-going use.

when walking from one end to the other. Popular with hirers they make ideal river craft, but their somewhat inelegant looks put off most private buyers.

Other specialist river craft include converted Dutch barges, but these are probably beyond the scope of the newcomer to boating.

Dayboats

Not everybody wants to spend long periods of time on their boat; many owners are happy to go out just for the day. A variety of craft are available for this purpose, ranging from the simple inflatable that can be rolled up and carried in the boot of the car through larger runabouts that need to be towed on a trailer and launched, up to the biggest boats that spend all their lives afloat. Inflatables and runabouts give you the flexibility of choosing a different cruising area each trip and will not incur any storage or mooring fees, but their facilities are limited. Larger craft up to 20ft or more can have cookers, fridges, canopies to keep the rain off, and even occasional berths for overnight stops. The smaller boats will be outboard powered, with the larger ones having inboard engines, either petrol or diesel – or even steam or electric propulsion. We will look at the latter in more detail in Chapter 6.

Licences

Whatever boat you use on a river, lake or canal will need a licence. Even if it is not permanently moored and you are putting it afloat just for the day, this will still apply. The licensing authority is often the local Regional Water Authority; if this is not the case, they will tell you who to contact. Costs vary, from a few pounds for small craft for short periods, up to £100 to £200 for the largest craft for a year, with different waters having different scales. Further details on licensing will be given in Chapter 10.

——— 3 ———
Sea-going cruisers

If you have decided that you want to do your boating at sea, a different set of conditions apply. The boat has to be bigger, stronger, faster, designed to take the waves, and better equipped. You and your crew have to be better prepared, both physically and mentally. You need to understand navigation, weather and boat handling, or have someone in your crew who does. However, none of these conditions is hard to achieve; they just need planning.

The rewards, in the view of most sea-going boaters, are well worth it. As you cast off from the land, you enter a different world. The hassle and rush of your daily life is left behind. The sea is the last uncluttered open space, and every boat is an island on it. You are in command and you make the decisions. Your safety and security depend on these decisions, but the responsibility is both exciting and rewarding. You plan your passages and have to take account of many factors – wind and waves, weather and tides – but when all the calculations come out right, and the correct buoy or harbour appears just where it should be, the satisfaction you feel cannot be matched in our normal everyday lives.

How far do you want to go?

This is probably the first decision you have to make when you are contemplating boating on the sea. At this point we will define the sea as any waters that are affected by the tide. They can be divided broadly into three categories, which make increasingly greater demands on boat and crew. The areas are: estuaries and harbours; coastal waters; and offshore or cross-Channel waters.

Estuaries and harbours

Estuaries and harbours are probably where most people start their sea-going boating. You will not normally be out of sight of land, buoys and navigational marks appear at regular intervals, and the waters are generally sheltered from heavy seas. This is not to say that these waters should not be respected, but with their shorter distances and more moderate sea conditions they make fewer demands on the skipper and crew and are ideal for learning the ropes. Popular locations in this category around Britain include The Thames Estuary, Chichester Harbour, The Solent, Poole Harbour, the River Dart, Falmouth Harbour, Milford Haven, and the River Clyde.

Boats suitable for these waters come in all different shapes and sizes, but for comfort it is not wise to go shorter than 16ft or preferably 18ft. You will need an engine capable of pushing the boat along at a minimum of 6 to 8 knots, with enough reserve power to overcome waves or a headwind. You should carry a back-up engine in case the main one should fail (though this is not essential) but you must have an adequate anchor. Safety equipment should as a minimum include lifejackets for all the

A sturdy 16ft boat with shelter forward, suitable for use in estuaries and harbours.

crew, plus flares and navigation lights; a hand-held VHF radio is a bonus. Navigation equipment should consist at least of up-to-date charts and compass, preferably also with an echo-sounder, speedometer and log.

Coastal waters

Your next step forward will be coastal trips. You will still mainly be in sight of land, but navigation marks will become less frequent. Looking at the coastline from the sea often does not tell you where you are, and bad visibility can obscure it completely, so you have to be able to plan your passage using instruments and charts. The traditional chart is still the basic starting point for all sea-going navigation, and understanding it is vital. You can learn how to navigate from books and magazines, from night schools, or by going on purpose-designed courses; these are described in more detail in Chapter 10. However, at this stage we have to stress the importance of knowing what you are doing, or having someone on board who does.

Essential instruments for coastal navigation include the compass, echo-sounder, speedometer and log mentioned above, plus a hand-bearing compass. Optional but useful items include electronic position-fixing devices, such as a Decca navigator or Loran set; radar for use at night or in poor visibility; and nowadays almost an essential, a VHF radio for talking to other vessels, harbours, and shore stations such as the coastguard.

Your boat will have to be bigger and sturdier to take the heavier seas you might encounter. Whilst even the smallest craft can undertake coastal trips in fine weather, this is not recommended for newcomers as conditions can deteriorate rapidly. We would suggest 21ft as a minimum and only for short trips, with preferably 23ft for comfortable short passages in settled weather and 27ft for longer passages. Of course these can only be generalizations, as different craft will be more or less seaworthy and different crews better or less able to handle the conditions. Our suggestion is that you graduate slowly to longer trips to enable you to get the measure of your boat's capabilities and to increase your confidence and that of your crew.

A back-up engine in case the main one should fail becomes even more important out at sea. This means that you should either have a spare in the form of an outboard that can be clamped on the transom or have a twin-engined boat. Whilst many single-engined craft do ply Britain's coastal waters, they depend upon being able to repair any breakdown that might occur on board. If that does not succeed they have to call for assistance, which for most people means the rescue services. However, at sea these are not the RAC or AA, ready to help you by the roadside; they are the volunteers of the RNLI (Royal National Lifeboat Institution) or similar services, whose purpose is to save lives not to look after badly prepared amateurs. So make sure you do not become another unwanted statistic.

Offshore waters

The final and most exciting step in your boating career is to go offshore or cross-Channel, out of the sight of land. For this you must be prepared for any eventuality. Your vessel must be well found, usually a minium of 30ft long, preferably with twin engines. You must allow for the possibility of encountering bad weather, which means even more careful planning and listening to forecasts. You must have enough experienced crew members on board to work a simple watch system – after three or four hours at sea, even the most experienced helmsman needs a

The Princess 315. A powerful flying-bridge planing cruiser capable of coastal and cross-Channel passages at up to 30 knots.

break. You must also be sure that enough people know how to handle the boat in the event of anything happening to the skipper. A life-raft now becomes an essential item of safety equipment – if the boat should sink, even if you get out a radio message, it could be several hours before help arrives.

It goes without saying that your navigation becomes even more critical offshore, as does the condition of the equipment on board. Essential systems should have backups – a hand-held VHF as well as a fixed set, charts and a Decca navigator. Certain engine spares are needed, including fuel filters, drive belts, a spare injector line and so on. And of course all the boat's paperwork must be in order – the bill of sale, proof of insurance, registration, plus preferably a certificate of competence for the skipper. All these preparations are covered in Chapter 10, but be sure to get them right. Overseas officialdom is notorious for needing everything in order. The reward for all this is still totally worth the trouble. To navigate your own vessel safely to a foreign port is one of the most exciting and satisfying things you can do.

How fast do you want to go?

This is the next question you have to ask before choosing your boat for the sea. Boats divide into two main categories, displacement and planing, defined by their hull shape and their maximum speed.

Displacement hulls

A displacement boat pushes its way through the water making a distinct wave at the bow and creating others along its length and one at the stern. Its maximum speed is limited by its waterline length, and can be approximately worked out by the formula $V = 1.3\sqrt{L}$ where V is the speed of the boat in knots and L is the waterline length in feet. Thus a boat 30ft long overall, whose waterline length is around 25ft, will have a maximum displacement speed of $1.3\sqrt{25}$, or 1.3×5, which is 6½ knots. Trying to

Section through a typical displacement or semi-displacement hull.

push the boat any faster will cause the bow to rise and the stern to dig in, and will create an even bigger wave but little more speed. The longer the boat the greater its displacement speed – the QE2 which is 900ft long on the waterline will have a theoretical maximum speed of $1.3\sqrt{900}$ or 1.3×30, which is 39 knots. A typical displacement boat will have rounded underwater sections.

Planing hulls

For a boat to travel faster than displacement speed, it has to partially lift out of the water and start travelling over its surface, rather than pushing through it. This is known as planing and will occur only if the hull is the right shape and there is sufficient power in reserve to get it over the first bow wave, or hump. A planing hull will have flat or vee-shaped bottom sections, and a distinct 'corner' where the bottom meets the sides, known as the chine. Once the boat is on the plane, which will occur between 10 to 15 knots depending on the shape of the bottom, it will level out. Theoretically its top speed is then limited only by the amount of power it is given. For practical purposes, planing cruisers usually have a top speed of between 20 and 30 knots. Sports cruisers and racing boats, of course, can go faster, with

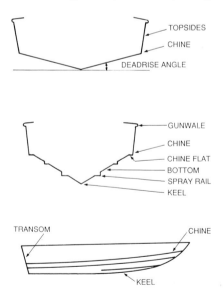

A typical planing hull.

top speeds of 50 knots for some pleasure boats and 100 knots or more for racing craft.

Planing hulls are further subdivided into categories that depend on the vee-angle of the bottom. This angle is more correctly termed the angle of deadrise, and it has important effects on the performance and sea-keeping of the boat.

The earliest planing boats had virtually flat bottoms, with 0° to 10° angles of deadrise, known as shallow vee. They planed easily with relatively low-powered engines and performed well in calm conditions. However, when driving into the wind, as the waves got higher they tended to slam or pound into them, requiring the boat to slow down.

The next step forward came with hulls whose deadrise was between 10° and 20°. This is known as medium vee, and the increasingly sharp bottom sections enabled the boats to cut into the waves better and go faster without slamming. However, the deeper vee gave a less efficient planing surface and required greater power to get over the hump and onto the plane.

The final development was the deep-vee hull, with a deadrise between 20° and 25°. Boats with this hull can maintain high speeds into the steepest of seas, and it is thus favoured by racing boats. Its drawback is the high power needed to get onto the plane and a high, bow-up running angle at slow speeds.

For practical purposes, most modern cruiser designs feature a combination of the above forms, with hulls whose deadrise amidships is greater than that at the transom, giving the wave-cutting qualities forward, where they are needed, with easier planing sections aft. These are known as modified vee hulls, or medium-to-deep vee. Typical designs will have a deadrise of 22° amidships and 18° at the transom.

Semi-displacement hulls

Also known as a semi-planing, this hull shape is a cross between the first two. Its bottom sections aft are close to flat, angling as they move forward, but the chine is rounded, not sharp. A semi-displacement boat's top speed is around 20 to 25 knots, but it uses more power than a pure planing boat at these speeds. Its advantages are that it can travel at intermediate speeds (around 18 knots) in rough sea conditions that would cause a planing boat to drop off the plane. Pilot boats and lifeboats use this hull form, but not many pleasure craft.

Pros and cons

So what are the benefits or detractions of the two systems? A planing boat needs more installed power to get it on the plane. Bigger engines are more expensive, take up more space and burn more fuel. Their advantage is that you get where you want to go much more quickly. At 25 knots a 50 mile journey takes two hours. At 8 knots in a displacement boat it will take you six hours, without taking account of the tide. If the tide turns against you with a flow of 2 knots you will be down to 6 knots and looking at an eight-hour journey. During this time the weather can change significantly, and you may end up finishing your trip in rough conditions or in the dark. A 2 knot tide against the planing boat, by contrast, will only decrease its speed to 23 knots, adding just ten minutes to the trip.

So you can see why in this hurry-everywhere age, in which most people's time is limited, planing boats are more popular. If you only have a weekend to go boating and must be back in the office by Monday morning, it is no good telephoning to say you encountered a foul tide around Beachy Head. And while the actual fuel costs for a journey will be greater, in your annual costs of running the boat, this will probably add only 10 to 20 per cent overall. On the other hand, a displacement boat will cost you less to buy in the first place, and if your funds are limited, this might allow you to buy a bigger boat than would otherwise have been possible. The other advantage of the displacement boat is that if the weather should get really bad, the slower vessel's hull design will often be better suited to plodding through the rough seas than that of its speedier rival, which will be forced to slow down so much that it will come off the plane.

Knots and miles per hour

This talk of speeds is an opportune moment to explain the curious nautical measure of the knot. A knot is defined as a speed of one nautical mile per hour. The nautical mile is not the same length as its land-based counterpart. It is slightly longer, at 6,060ft, compared to the statute mile's 5,280ft, because a nautical mile is defined as the distance covered by one minute of latitude on the Earth's surface. 60 minutes make up a degree of latitude, and there are 360 degrees from the North Pole, round to the South Pole and back again, making 21,600 nautical miles in all. Thus the circumference of the Earth via the Poles is 21,600 nautical miles, or 24,800 statute miles. Why mariners use the nautical mile becomes clear when you study navigation and see the logic of having distances measured relative to latitude.

In practical terms, 1 knot is approximately 1.15 mph. Thus a boat whose speed is quoted as 10 knots will be moving at 11.5mph, at 20 knots will be progressing at 23mph, and so on. When you travel on inland waters, however, it is more logical to describe speeds in miles per hour, as the surrounding land will be measured in statute miles.

In America boat speeds are usually quoted in miles per hour because much of their boating is on inland waters. Around the rest of the world, speeds on inland waters are usually in kilometres per hour (kph), but out at sea you will find yourself back to knots. So the anachronistic knot does have another value; it provides an international measure of speed.

. . . and gallons

One more quirk of the marine measuring system is gallons. The US gallon is smaller than its British counterpart by a factor of 20 per cent. Thus 1 Imp gal = 1.2 US gal, 5 Imp gal = 6 US gal. Beware of this when examining quoted tank capacities or fuel consumptions in American brochures. A full table of comparative weights and measures will be found in Appendix 4.

Examples of sea-going craft

Having described the basic types of boats that can go to sea we shall take a look at a few typical and popular models on the market.

For estuary and harbour use a trailable boat is ideal, and one of the all-time favourites over the years has been the Shetland Family Four. Eighteen feet long, it has a cabin forward with double berth, table, small galley and portable toilet. Out in the cockpit you can sleep two children under the canopy or seat four adults for the day. For fishing, pottering, sunbathing or even waterskiing if you have a big enough engine, this is the ideal starter boat. An outboard motor provides the power; up to 20hp if you are content to travel at displacement speeds of up to 7 knots, or 50–90hp if you want to plane at between 20 and 30 knots. The price new will be around £6,000, with the engine costing another £2,000 to £4,000 depending on power. A suitable road trailer will cost a further £1,000. Second-hand you can expect to pay between 50 to 75 per cent of these prices.

If you want to travel farther down the coast a Sealine 255, or its bigger brother the 285, would be ideal. It contains a main saloon forward with a settee and table that convert to a double berth, plus a separate double cabin aft that runs under the cockpit. An enclosed toilet with full-standing headroom has a sink and shower, both with running hot-and-cold water, while the WC will discharge into the sea. The galley has a gas cooker with a two-burner hob, oven and grill, and an electric fridge. Out in the cockpit there is room for six to eight people to soak up the sun or swim from the integral aft bathing platform. Power comes from outdrive engines, usually twin petrols between 200 and 450hp total, though single installations and diesel engines are available. Speeds will be between 25–40 knots maximum, depending on the engine size chosen, and prices are from around £30,000 to £45,000.

Another approach is that adopted by the Scandinavians. There the aft cabin, centre-cockpit layout is popular, typified by boats in the Nimbus range. The cockpit is a sheltered all-

The 17ft Shetland Family Four is a popular trailable starter boat suitable for use on rivers or sheltered estuaries and harbours. It provides berths for two adults in the cabin and possibly for two children in the cockpit.

weather area, with a sun-roof for fine days but a hard-top to keep off the rain and spray. The galley is located there rather than down in the cabin, keeping the cook in contact with the rest of the party. You can also eat in the cockpit, though a table in the cabin allows you to batten down the hatches on really cold days. In this respect diesel-fired central heating is a boon. The aft double cabin allows a second couple to sleep on board with complete privacy, while a third cabin tucked under the cockpit will take children or occasional guests. Power usually comes from a single 200hp diesel engine giving an economical 20 to 24 knots, though other models in the Nimbus range are available with twin installations. A new Nimbus 2600 or 3003 will cost you £55,000 to £75,000.

The third layout commonly found on sea-going boats is that of the flying bridge and aft cockpit. As its name implies a flying bridge, or fly bridge as it is sometimes known, is a raised driving position built on top of the main cabin or saloon. Located there are a steering wheel and instruments, usually duplicates of those in the wheelhouse below though sometimes less extensive,

From Sweden, the Nimbus 3003 has an aft cabin, giving it six berths, and is capable of both river trips and sea-going use at up to 24 knots.

plus seating for three or more passengers depending on boat size. Driving up on the fly bridge lets you be out in the sunshine and the best of the weather. You also have an excellent all around view, important when travelling at speed or when manœuvring at close quarters in the marina. You are clear of the spray that can be thrown up even on fine days, and if the design of the screen is right you will also be sheltered from the wind. Less obvious but no less important – you will be further away from the engines. No matter how well they are sound-proofed, powerful engines, particularly diesels, are noisy, and this can be wearing after a while. Up on the flying bridge you are removed from the noise of both the engine room and the exhausts.

A typical fly bridge boat is the Princess 315 (see page 28). The upper level will take the driver and three passengers, while down in the cockpit you can entertain four or five more. Inside in the saloon is a settee and table that convert to a double berth, while opposite is another single settee/berth. Forward is a private double cabin. In between is the galley with three-burner hob, oven, fridge and plenty of storage space, while opposite is the toilet compartment. All the accommodation has at least 6ft of headroom. The lower helm position is sited at the forward end of the saloon. (Most fly bridge boats come with the lower helm as standard – a few American boats show it as an extra, as it never seems to rain there!) Power is provided by a pair of 200hp diesel engines, either inboard mounted under the saloon or with outdrives. Maximum speed will be around 27 to 30 knots, and the price is from £85,000. With this boat you can happily undertake coastal or cross-Channel trips.

If you want more accommodation you will have to go up in size, with 35ft giving you a second or third private cabin and six or more berths.

If all this high-speed boating is not for you, a displacement craft could fit your bill. The acknowledged experts in this field are the Dutch, and their sturdy, steel-built cruisers are ideal both for river or sea-going use. A typical range is that of Pedro Boats; the Pedro 30 is the ideal starter craft. Accommodation comprises a double cabin aft, enclosed toilet, saloon amidships with a settee that can convert to a double berth, galley forward, and a second double cabin ahead of that, with two singles or one double berth. Power comes from a single 62hp diesel engine giving 6 to 7 knots, and the price starts at around £45,000. a second engine will add approximately £11,000 to the price, and while it will not give any significant increase in speed it will give you peace of mind if you want to undertake longer passages.

4

Inflatables, runabouts and funboats

The cheapest and easiest way to get afloat is with a runabout or inflatable. Thousands of people take to the water this way every year, and the reasons are obvious. The initial cost is lower, running costs are low, and you have the convenience of being able to choose a different cruising ground every time you go on the water. Transport is also simplified – a runabout can be towed on a trailer behind the average family saloon, while an inflatable can either be carried on the roof or (deflated) in the boot. This means you can take it with you on holiday or for weekend trips. So let's take a closer look at the choices.

Inflatables

The modern inflatable is a strong, sturdy piece of equipment. We are not talking here about plastic beach toys, but purpose-designed boats. Today's materials and construction methods ensure that you will get many years of useful life from these craft, and Avon, for instance, gives a ten-year guarantee for the material of its products.

The tubes are normally made from a composite material comprising a fabric backed by a proofing medium. The latter is usually neoprene rubber, but sometimes polyurethane or similar compounds are used. The strength and durability of the material is usually dependent on its weight and hence its cost; some manufacturers offer different ranges made from different grades of material, with consequent cost variations.

In this context, remember that you will likely graduate from your inflatable to a larger craft and will need a tender for it, so extra money spent on this purchase will prove a benefit in years to come as the dinghy will still have useful life left. This consideration should also have a bearing on the size of craft you choose.

The smallest inflatables are around 8ft long. They will take two adults confortably, but their use is limited by the size. The next step up is 10ft, and this makes a good all-around boat. Two adults and one or two small children will fit for river use, while the boat can also be used occasionally in sheltered harbours provided you do not overload it. For more frequent use on the sea, 12ft to 14ft boats are preferable.

For slow speed, non-planing use (between 4 and 5 knots) a 2hp outboard motor is adequate for the smallest model, with 4hp giving more push on larger versions that may be more heavily laden, and for use in rougher, windier conditions. To achieve planing performance at 10 to 20 knots you will require a 6–10hp engine for an 8–10ft boat with two people in it. For a 12–14ft boat you will need 10–25hp and will be able to carry four people at up to 25 knots.

Inflatables are fine in sheltered waters and smooth seas, but if it should get at all choppy they will give you a hard, bouncy ride, with a lot of spray. This may be fine for trained lifeboat crews but rapidly becomes tiresome for ordinary mortals.

Each occupant should always wear a lifejacket or buoyancy aid. Note that there is an important difference between the two.

This Flatacraft Force 3 RIB will give you plenty of fun on its own and also makes an excellent tender for boats longer than 30ft.

A buoyancy aid, usually of the waistcoat style, provides support to wearers in the water but assumes they are conscious all the time. If they are unconscious it will not turn them over if they should fall face down in the water, nor will it hold their head above the water. A full lifejacket, on the other hand, has more buoyancy and has a buoyant collar to keep you floating face up, with your mouth out of the water.

Buoyancy aids are generally considered suitable for river and canal use and in dinghies and runabouts for people who can swim. For nonswimmers and children, even in rivers, a lifejacket is a better alternative, while out at sea it is essential. A lifejacket can either have permanent foam for part of its buoyancy, topped up with air by mouth for the remainder, or it can be totally air filled, either by mouth or by a miniature emergency CO_2 cylinder. The all-air types fold up small enough that they can be worn completely unobtrusively when not in use without restricting your movements.

Rigid-hull inflatables

Half-way between inflatables and runabouts come the rigid-hull inflatable boats (RIBs). As their name implies, these feature a solid GRP hull bonded to inflatable tubes around the gunwale.

An Avon 4m Sea Rider RIB, capable of 30 knots and holding up to four people.

The rigid hull gives a vastly superior performance to an all-rubber boat in waves, enabling the boat to be driven fast in rough conditions, while the rubber tube gives superb buoyancy should you hit an extra large wave. For this reason they are the chosen vessel of lifeboat and rescue teams, used in the severest of weathers. These safe and fast features also make them excellent pleasure boats, with the added benefit that the rubber tubes will not damage another craft as they come alongside. They are therefore frequently used as tenders for larger craft, where their final benefit – the fact that they are lightweight – comes to the fore.

The smallest RIBs are around 10ft long, and these, loaded with two people, will give planing performance at 10 to 20 knots with as little as 10hp. The maximum engine you are likely to want to fit is 15hp, and at this power you should consider fitting wheel steering and remote throttle controls which will give you safer control of the engine. They also allow you to sit further forward in the boat, with your weight helping to keep the bow down – an advantage in waves.

At 12ft the RIB will take a 30–40hp engine and give up to 30 to 35 knots. It will often have seats and a windscreen and will carry

A Sea Ray 18 outboard runabout with bow-rider forward seating area.

four people. Fifteen feet is generally the largest pleasure boat size in RIBs, taking four to six passengers at up to 35 knots with up to 70hp. Beyond this and you are into the rescue-style boat, with a central, motor-cycle type seat which allows you to drive the boat fast in rough conditions with the worst of the shock as you hit the waves being taken by your legs.

Runabouts

Sometimes called sports boats these are all-GRP, with seats and windscreens and varying degrees of equipment that can include radios and even a cushioned area under the bow for overnight sleeping. A folding cockpit cover may be supplied to keep off the rain.

A runabout will have more room in it than a RIB, with no inflatable tubes taking up the space. It will also be more luxurious, with carpet on the floor and usually some lockers to take loose items and gear. It also looks more like a 'real' boat and for these reasons will continue to prove popular with many people.

Normal sizes run from around 14ft, which will take a 40–80hp engine and give 20 to 30 knots, through 16ft with 60–90hp, right up to 19–21ft, with from 100hp up to 200hp or more and top speeds of up to 50 knots. In the larger sizes you will tend to find an inboard petrol engine fitted, driving through a stern drive, rather than an outboard. The advantages of the inboard are less noise, better fuel consumption, and more reliability. It is also less vulnerable to being stolen. Disadvantages are its greater weight and a higher initial cost.

A variant of the runabout that has come from America is the bow-rider boat. Instead of a solid GRP foredeck with a one-piece windscreen, this has an open cockpit forward with seating all round, and a three-piece windscreen with a centre section that hinges out of the way to allow you to walk through. The bow rider thus has extra space for passengers or for lounging in the sun. Care must be taken, though, that people are not sitting in the bow area when you are travelling at planing speeds. If the boat should hit an unexpected wave or wash, they will be thrown about and possibly injured. Also, you should fit a canvas cover over the open bow when you are travelling at sea or in rough conditions, in case a wave should come over and swamp the boat.

Equipping your boat

If you are going to be using your runabout or RIB at sea, or in fact in anything but the most sheltered of rivers, you should carry certain safety equipment. A pump is obvious, with preferably both an electric model and a manual one as a back-up, or even just a bucket as an emergency spare. You should carry as many lifejackets or buoyancy aids as you are likely to have passengers. It is your responsibility to ensure the safety of your crew, and the lifejackets should be easily accessible. A paddle, or preferably two, is something you might not have considered, but it should be carried. Engines can break down, or you could run out of fuel and find yourself drifting onto rocks or other dangers. It is surprising how much headway you can make with a paddle, often enough to stem the current. An anchor with 80–90ft of line is also important. This will also keep you from being blown too far by the wind in the event of breakdown, or being carried onto rocks. It is also very handy for sunbathing, fishing or swimming in a secluded cove. If you are going to sea, flares should be carried; your chandler will be able to advise you of a suitable inshore pack. Again, if you are using your boat at sea you should have a chart of the area, plus a compass. The chart will enable you to avoid running aground, while the compass will help you find your way home if fog should come down or you are caught out in the dark. A hand-held VHF radio may seem something of a luxury, but it will give you peace of mind and enable you to call for help in an emergency.

Waterskiing

When the novelty of skimming across the waves in your boat has worn off and you are bored with sunbathing, a set of waterskis could be the next answer. Most runabouts and RIBs above 12ft will tow a waterskier, though the performance will be dependent on the size of the motor on the boat. Powers at the top end of the ranges we have suggested will be necessary to get a person of average weight up on twin skis, while even more pull will be needed for mono skiing. It is essential for safety reasons that you always have a second person in the boat to act as an observer. The driver should concentrate at all times on what is ahead, allowing the second person to tell him if the skier has fallen off or is in difficulties. The observer can also keep an eye on where the skier is in the water, enabling the boat to safely return to pick him or her up.

Funboats

Also called Personal Recreational Vehicles, in the inevitable American jargon, these include the whole family of jet-skis, wet-bikes, powered surfboards, and so on. Increasingly popular with their owners, they are unfortunately gaining a reputation with other water users as the hooligan element of boating. Many foreign countries have imposed stringent restrictions on where these craft can be used, with speed limits and exclusion zones close to beaches.

Used responsibly, however, funboats offer the most thrilling action on the water. You have to be prepared to be cold and wet, and in Britain some sort of wetsuit is a must at most times of the year. Most of these craft have room for only one person on board, though some more sophisticated models will carry two.

Funboats usually drive by means of a water jet connected to a two-stroke petrol engine. This avoids exposed propellers that could injure the driver if he or she should fall off. Steering is done either by turning the jet or by leaning your body to one side or the other. If you should fall off, the throttle automatically closes and the boat circles around slowly, allowing you to intercept it and climb back on board.

The Kawasaki Jet-Ski is a funboat for those who don't mind getting wet!

——— 5 ———
Trailer boats
and trailing

If funds are low but you still want to get afloat, the answer for many people is a trailer boat. In fact, if you were to talk to owners of larger cruisers you would find that many of them – the author included – first started out on the water this way.

The advantages are cost (the boat itself will be cheaper and you have no mooring charges) and convenience (you can choose a different cruising ground every weekend, or settle on one that is near to home for most of the year, going further afield for your holidays).

Trailer boats divide into runabouts, with open cockpits and no accommodation, and cruisers, with two or four berths depending on their size. The latter can be surprisingly sophisticated, offering a comfortable home for weekends or longer trips. The limit to how large a boat you can trail is governed by the size of your car, so we will look at this in detail now.

Towing regulations

The laws regarding towing are covered in two large Department of Transport volumes called *Construction and Use Regulations*. These cover every aspect of vehicle law, with towing under just one section. You will rarely have to consult these unless you have an exceptional or abnormally large load and are looking for the final word.

Instead we recommend you purchase a copy of *Guide to Trailers & Towing* published by Indespension Ltd. Indespension are one of the largest suppliers of trailers in the UK, with units that will cater for everything from horses to boats to goods, and their manual has become something of a bible on the subject. The latest edition at time of writing costs £3.50 and is available from their dealers, who can be found in *Yellow Pages*. In addition to covering the regulations the manual details all the Indespension components and spares available and provides many helpful hints on towing. Some of the basic points you need to know follow.

Towing weight

The first question you need to ask is how much your car will tow, and then how heavy is the boat that you are thinking of buying. Maximum towing weight is governed by the kerb-side weight and power of your car. Kerb-side weight is defined as the weight of the car with a full fuel tank but no passengers or load.

If the trailer has no brakes the maximum permissible towing load – which includes boat, trailer and gear – is 50 per cent of the kerb-side weight of the car, with an overall maximum of 750kg. If the trailer has brakes the maximum recommended towing load is stipulated by the car manufacturer. This will take into account the weight of the car plus the power of the engine. The rule of thumb used to be that the maximum recommended

This 4m Flatacraft RIB can be trailed behind the smallest car.

towing load equalled the kerb-side weight of the car. For comfortable towing over long distances this was reduced to 80 per cent of the kerb-side weight to give a margin of power in reserve. The situation today has been complicated by the number of different engine sizes and power options available in a given vehicle, giving rise to different recommended maximum loads. Thus a Cavalier, with a kerb-side weight of 1,020kg, has a recommended maximum of 1,000kg in its 1.4 litre version, 1,200kg for the 1.6, and 1,350kg for the 2.0 litre.

In practice, the best advice is to use the 1:1 ratio as a basic rule of thumb but to check in your owner's manual for the precise figure. From this you will see that typical maximum towing weights for cars range from 500kg for a Nova, for instance, up to 1,700kg for a large saloon such as a Senator. More weight than this and you will have to move into the Land Rover bracket.

It is important to adhere to these figures for practical reasons (too heavy, and you will be the snail at the head of a frustrated convoy, with no power in reserve, and you will experience impaired braking and handling) and legal ones (in the event of your being stopped or involved in an accident, you could be prosecuted or find your insurance invalid).

Brakes

Brakes on a trailer normally take the form of the overrun variety. As you apply the car brakes the trailer tends to catch up, compressing a spring or hydraulic damper in the coupling head, which in turn automatically applies the trailer brakes. It is essential that the braking mechanism be correctly set up, otherwise you will experience snatching or poor braking effect every time you slow down. A dealer is the best person to set up the brakes correctly, but you can do it yourself by varying the adjustment and checking the effect.

It cannot be stressed how important the brakes are. You are effectively doubling the weight of your car hence, if the trailer brakes are not working correctly, you could be doubling your stopping distance. Even with a well-adjusted rig you must make allowance for the extra weight and drive more cautiously. This applies not only to stopping but also to cornering, particularly on roundabouts, and accelerating – allow much more distance when overtaking and when pulling away at a junction.

When you reverse, the action of compressing the towing head tends to apply the trailer brakes, bringing the whole rig to a stop. Old trailers had a lock that you had to get out of the car to apply when about to reverse. Modern models are fitted with auto-reverse brakes, which overcome this problem. Not only are these a convenience, but from April 1989 they became mandatory, enabling you to reverse quickly in an emergency.

A trailer must also be fitted with a hand-brake, capable of holding it on a slope of 18 per cent. When towing, this hand-brake lever must be connected by a wire or chain to a fixed part of the car. In the event of the tow hitch breaking, or disengaging, the wire will apply the brake, bringing the trailer to a stop.

Speeds

The maximum speed with a trailer in the UK is 50mph on a single-carriageway road and 60mph on a dual-carriageway or motorway, assuming that no lower limit is in force. Additionally, you are not allowed to travel in the outside lane of a three-lane motorway or in the outside two lanes of a four-lane road.

Lights

Trailer lights are connected as extensions to the existing car lights. Leads are run from the rear lighting circuits to a seven-pin socket permanently mounted on the tow bar. This matches a seven-pin plug on the trailer. Most boat trailers have all their lights mounted on a portable board which can be removed when the boat is launched into the water. These boards are best bought ready assembled – making your own is hardly ever worth it. Ensure that the seven-core cable with the board is long enough to reach easily the back of the car, as they are often too short for larger boats.

The lights that the law requires are, in general, the same as those on the rear of the car. The exceptions are reversing lights, which are not compulsory, and rear fog lights – only one is compulsory, even if the car has two. Additional markers required include two reflective red triangles, orange side reflectors if the trailer exceeds a certain length, and front white lights if it exceeds a certain width.

In order that the flashers operate at the required rate, a heavy-duty flasher unit normally needs to be fitted, together with a secondary repeater light on the car dashboard to show you that the trailer indicators are working. This repeater can be replaced by a bleeper in the rear of the car, avoiding the need to run a cable forward, but personally we find that this rapidly becomes annoying, particularly to rear-seat passengers.

In general, you should look after the trailer lights and every time you reconnect them get someone to check that they are all operational before driving away. There is nothing more dangerous than a trailer with only one rear light, or indicators that do not work.

Number plates

A number plate in the same style as car plates, black letters on yellow reflective ground, must be fitted, with the same registration as the towing car. It is sensible to have one made up, then carry it permanently in the boot of the car.

Tyres

The normal car regulations regarding tread depth and wear apply to trailer tyres. Cross-ply or radial tyres can be fitted, regardless of what tyres are on the car, but you cannot mix the two types on one axle. Trailer tyres have to be suitable for the load they are to carry – often they have to be heavier duty than equivalent car sizes because they may be carrying greater loads, especially if the trailer has two wheels rather than four. Tyre pressures are also usually higher than on the car – consult the tyre manufacturer on this point, telling them what the maximum load will be and on how many wheels.

General

The maximum gross towing weight of the trailer (including boat) must be marked clearly on its nearside at the front. The kerb-side weight of the car should also be displayed inside the nearside of the windscreen. These enable police to check that you are not breaking the law.

Insurance: Your existing car insurance normally will cover you for third-party risks when towing, but it will not necessarily provide comprehensive cover for the trailer or boat. Check this point with your company.
Driving licence: A full driving licence is necessary when towing. A provisional licence is not sufficient.
Tax: No additional road tax is required for a private vehicle towing a trailer.

Mirrors: A nearside mirror is compulsory if the view to the rear through the interior mirror is obscured by the boat. Fitting one is sensible anyway, to allow you to judge the width of the trailer.

Towing overseas

Different countries have different regulations on towing, and you should check these before you set off. The Indespension manual covers this; alternatively talk to the RAC or AA.

Towing techniques

Towing requires you to follow certain techniques before you set out and while you are on your way. It is essential that you adhere to these principles at all times. They are not difficult to master, but it is easy to forget them after a long journey.

Loading

Locating the boat correctly on the trailer is essential. It should be positioned fore-and-aft such that there is always a down load on the tow hitch. The maximum permissible nose weight is given by the car manufacturer, but a minimum of 25kg is necessary with a maximum usually around 50kg. With too little down load,

The Sea Ray 21 sports boat will need a large saloon to tow it.

or an actual up load, the trailer will move like a snake at speed. This snaking can start as low as 40mph, though more often it will occur at 50–60mph. Snaking can become uncontrollable, particularly if you have to swerve or brake suddenly. Passing a high-sided vehicle can also initiate snaking. The correct nose weight will eliminate the problem, or delay its onset until well above the legal limit.

Loose items should be secured in the boat, preferably located as near to amidships as possible. To reduce the weight of the trailer it is often preferable to carry heavy weights in the car, though take care not to overload the rear suspension. Try to wait till the end of the journey to fill up the boat fuel tanks.

Tying down

The boat should be securely lashed down. The best system for this is ratchet-tightened webbing straps, since they always maintain tension and will not slacken. However well you tie rope it will always loosen, and it is also more likely to chafe the boat. Belt-and-braces is the best principle for securing a boat: Do not just rely on the winch at the bow – use a rope there as well; do not use just one strap – use two, plus a rope to back them up. Remember, as the driver you are responsible for the load, so for peace of mind do all the lashing yourself, or at least check the work of others.

Small outboard motors are best taken off the transom while towing and carried either well secured in the boat or in the car boot. Larger engines should be partially tilted up, with the load taken either by a wooden chock or wedge, or by the power trim. Do not tow with the engine raised in its fully tilted position, as it will exert enormous strain on the bracket and the transom. The propeller and skeg should be protected to prevent injury to pedestrians and cyclists, and they should be clearly visible if they project behind the lighting board. The best way to achieve both of these is with one of the orange PVC bags sold for the purpose.

Driving

The most important point is always to remember that you have a trailer behind you, particularly in familiar roads and situations. Most people who tow can recall with anguish the occasion when they pulled into a petrol station or car park, and clipped the pump or the next car with the trailer wheel. If you are lucky it is only your pride that is dented; if you are not it can be expensive.

The basic points to remember when you are turning are: cut too close and the trailer will clip the kerb or a parked car. Take the curve too wide, and the back of the trailer can swing out and hit an overtaking car. Before your first journey, some practice in an empty car park works wonders. Do this without the boat on the trailer so that you can watch what the back is doing, but add a couple of lengths of timber to show you where the extremities of the boat would be. Set up some carboard boxes to simulate corners and other cars.

The same session should include the *bête noire* of towing – reversing. This is the one manœuvre that reduces all drivers to the same common denominator and can bring strong men to tears. The basic principle to remember is that to start the turn, you move the wheel in apparently the opposite direction to which you want the trailer to go. Then when the trailer is turning satisfactorily, straighten up the wheel and apply some opposite lock to prevent it swinging around too far and jack-knifing.

Always try to start the manœuvre with the car and trailer in a straight line, and do not be afraid to abandon the turn if it is going wrong, driving forward to get back to the straight-line position. In severely restricted conditions it is often simplest to unhook the trailer and manhandle it part or all of the way. Be careful if you do this on sloping ground or a slipway, as you can easily lose control.

Manual or automatic

Inexperienced towers shy away from automatic cars in the belief that they have less power than those with a manual gearbox. Drivers who have tried both know that the opposite is usually the case. The real towing power is the torque which the engine produces, and an automatic will always win here. Pulling away from rest, the torque convertor of the automatic gives the effect of a lower gear ratio, allowing you to take off faster and start on steeper slopes. Out on the road the automatic will shift down faster when you need it, leaving you to concentrate on the extra problems of the longer and wider load. The automatic gives precision control while manœuvring on a slipway, allowing you to inch forwards or backwards, with no revving engines or burning clutch and no hand-brake hill starts. The greater control over power also reduces the chance of wheel spin or digging in the tyres. Finally, if you have ever experienced one of our now inevitable three-mile motorway jams on a hot summer's afternoon in a manual car with a heavy boat behind, your left leg will soon cry out for a clutchless car.

Fuel consumption

Be prepared for extra fuel consumption with the boat behind. A medium-size cruiser towed fast will reduce your mileage from 30mpg to 20mpg or worse if it is heavily loaded. This can catch you low on fuel, especially on some of Britain's worse-served roads or in remote areas on a Sunday. It can also force you to use a garage with a small and crowded forecourt, which can be a problem to negotiate with a boat behind.

Launching and recovery

A whole chapter could be written on this subject, but a few tips are worth noting. The first is that the new generation of roller-type trailers really do work. They are more expensive, but they allow you to launch and recover with far more ease than the traditional flat-support type. If you are not super fit or blessed with a large strong family, invest in one of these for a quiet life.

The next common problem is getting the car stuck on a slippery ramp or with its wheels in mud or shingle. One way to avoid this is to let the trailer down on a long rope, keeping the car on the firm ground. For this to be successful, however, the rope must be substantial – at least 12mm in diameter or it will simply

The Hallmark Roller Coaster trailer helps you launch and recover from any slipway.

stretch and possibly break, with disastrous consequences. Also be aware that the front of the trailer can rear up unexpectedly when the boat is half on or off the trailer.

If the unwanted has already happened and your car is stuck or does not have the traction to pull the trailer up the ramp, getting an assist tow from another vehicle often works. Most modern cars have emergency towing eyes hidden behind cover plates in their front and rear bumpers. Do not use the bumper itself. If you can, site the second car on flat ground so that it does not have to pull its own weight uphill, but in all cases keep the length of the joining rope as short as possible. Work out in advance your plan of action and agree on signals. It is usually best if the lead car takes up the load first, with the stuck car letting in power gradually to avoid spinning its wheels and digging in further.

In serious cases, if extra traction is needed the lead car should be facing up the hill if it is rear-wheel drive or backing up the hill if it is front-wheel drive, but if its driving wheels are on hard ground this normally will be unnecessary.

Finally, if this chapter so far has sounded too doom laden, do not be put off. With proper preparation, trailer boating is straightforward and fun and gives an added dimension to boating. A well-rehearsed launch or recovery is not difficult to achieve and receives admiring nods from the slipway spectators. And if it should go wrong, don't take it too seriously.

Trailer boats

We will take a brief look here at the various types of boat suitable for trailing. Most of them will have been covered in detail elsewhere in the book, so we will only look at their towing features.

The simplest towable boat is the outboard-powered runabout. A typical 14ft example will weigh around 100kg empty. Add on 100kg for a 40hp engine with battery and controls, and 75kg for fuel, equipment and gear, and you have 275kg. A trailer to carry this will itself weigh 150kg, making 425kg total, suitable for the smallest car. At this weight you can often get away with an unbraked trailer if your car is double the weight, though brakes will give extra peace of mind behind the smallest cars.

A 16ft runabout will probably have a 60–75hp engine and a total boat and engine weight of 350–400kg. Add on 200kg for the trailer and you have a gross towing weight of 550–600kg. At this point you will almost certainly need a braked trailer, but it still should be easily towable behind almost any car.

If you are looking for a boat with some accommodation you will need a boat of around 17–18ft with an empty weight of around 600kg. Engine power to achieve planing performance will be 60–80hp, weighing around 150kg. Add on the inevitable equipment and gear, and you could have total boat weight of 800–900kg. A trailer to carry this will weigh 350kg, giving you a gross towing weight of 1,150–1,250kg. At this point you will have moved out of a small car's towing capability and will need at least a 1600cc family saloon.

You will also have reached the point where you have to decide on a two-wheel or four-wheel trailer. Two-wheel trailers are lighter, cheaper, and easier to move around when disconnected from the car. Their usual maximum carrying capacity is around 1,000kg. A four-wheel trailer, on the other hand, will take larger boats, usually from 750kg upwards. It is more stable to tow at speed, and it has added safety in that should a tyre blow out it will remain level while you come to a stop. It is, however, more expensive, and somewhat more cumbersome to manœuvre by hand.

The probable maximum size for a towable boat behind a car is 20–21ft, and even for this you will need the largest of saloons, as the total boat weight will be 1,200–1,300kg, and the gross towing weight 1,500–1,600kg. Beyond this, as we have said, you must drive a Land Rover or its equivalent.

——— 6 ———
Electric, steam, and traditional boats

The upsurge of interest in the traditional and a more relaxed approach to life has made itself felt in the boating world. Wooden craft are coming back into popularity, particularly on rivers and lakes. At the same time, increased environmental concern has prompted a new look at electric and steam propulsion.

Electric boats

It may come as some surprise that there is nothing new about electric power for boats. At the turn of the century, electricity was the favoured form of propulsion for river boats. The alternatives were steam, which was cumbersome, dirty and slow to start up, or the fledgling internal-combustion engine, which was heavy, unreliable and dangerous. Gradually petrol and diesel engines improved, and by the end of the First World War they reigned supreme and were to do so for the next sixty years.

Now we are again looking at electricity. The benefits are obvious: virtually no noise, pollution or vibration. It requires minimal maintenance and is clean. Against this are the cost and weight of the battery installation, limited power and range and the problems of finding a recharging point.

A boat starts off with the advantage of not having to go up hills, so the weight of the battery bank is not a major problem. In fact many boats already carry ballast to make them more stable and to keep the propeller fully immersed, so to a degree the batteries can simply replace ballast. The high initial cost of the batteries has to be viewed in terms of their overall life, say ten years, plus the savings in fuel over that period. The batteries used must be of the deep-cycle type, either normal duty or the heavier duty traction batteries for cases in which the installation will be used on a daily basis, such as in hire fleets.

Even with a large bank of batteries power will be low compared to that of an internal-combustion engine, so hulls must be long and slender to give an easy drive. At the same time, expectations of speed must be tempered. This is not a problem on rivers and canals, where you will be very popular travelling at modest speeds of 4–6mph, and regularly occurring locks mean that you always catch up with your faster, wave-making rivals anyway.

The power of an electric motor is measured in watts (W), with 1000 watts making 1 kilowatt (kW). 775 watts equals 1hp, and a typical motor for a 21ft dayboat will be 1.4kW, or around 2hp. Thus you can see how little power is needed to push a boat along at modest speeds. It is only when you strive for that extra 1–2 mph that you push up the power required. Estimates indicate that a 45ft narrowboat will need around 3–4kW to travel at 3–4mph, which is the normal canal speed, with 5–6kW allowing a reserve for manoeuvring and travelling into strong winds.

Your range will be limited by the capacity of the battery bank. Once this is exhausted you can go no further. Most installations aim for a running time of between 5 and 10 hours. Allowing for the fact that the engine will be stopped when you are in a lock, this will provide 1–2 days cruising between charges. For a dayboat that will always be returning to its base this is fine, but for longer cruises you must be sure you can find a suitable charging point every night. At present there is no guarantee of this, which holds many people back from converting to electric propulsion.

Various authorities have discussed the question of installing charging points at regular intervals along the waterways, but at the time of writing little progress has been made. In fact one of the schemes already in place has recently been abandoned due to lack of demand. Thus we have a chicken-and-egg situation where boat owners will not install electric propulsion until there are sufficient charging points, and charging points won't be installed until more boats convert to electric motors.

The way to provide a practical solution during the transition period is to use hybrid installations, in which the electric power plant is back up by a petrol or diesel engine. This engine can either drive the propeller directly, enabling you to carry on cruising until you reach a charging point, or will power a generator, allowing you to recharge the batteries yourself.

One way or another the change is bound to take place. By the year 2000 it is inconceivable that we will still allow noisy, polluting, internal-combustion engines on our inland waterways. Some European countries are already moving towards prohibiting them, with bans on two-stroke outboard motors on some lakes because of their excessive pollution and outright bans on internal-combustion engines on others.

If you do not wish to go to the expense and complication of a fixed inboard electrical power plant, it is still possible to go electric boating in small craft using electric outboard motors. These were originally developed in America as a secondary means of propulsion for small fishing boats. The main engine, a petrol outboard, is used to get out across the lake quickly to the best fishing grounds. Once there, the electric 'trolling' motor is used to stalk the fish silently. These units are of low output – a maximum of 300 watts normally, equivalent to ½hp – but they will power a small dinghy or punt.

Power can come from a single heavy-duty battery of around 100 ampere hours (Ah), which will give 3–4 hours running time depending on speed. Better still would be a pair of 75Ah batteries. These would be lighter to carry individually and would give an improved range. The maximum speed you could expect

An electric outboard motor on a dinghy is the simplest way of enjoying the waterways at their peaceful best.

from this combination would be 3–4mph, but this should be sufficient for a quiet afternoon's picnicking.

And quiet is the operative word with electric propulsion. Until you have sampled the joys of travelling on the waterways making no more noise than the wildlife around you, you cannot believe the difference it makes. Once you have done it, you wonder why you ever put up with an internal-combustion engine.

Steam boats

Along with the revival of interest in traditional craft has come a resurgence in the popularity of steam propulsion. The steam engine has none of the problems of shortage of power of its electric rivals. Up to 20hp or more is readily available, with sea-going vessels having plants of several thousand horsepower. Fuel is also carried easily, usually in the form of coal. The problems come with cost (a 20hp engine and boiler can cost up to £20,000 or more, due to being virtually hand-built these days) and convenience. Lighting the fire and getting up steam can take half an hour or more, and it is not a clean operation for either the people on board or those on adjoining boats. Black smuts are not welcome on pristine white decks or covers.

For the connoisseur, a steam launch is the ultimate river boat.

One solution to the problems of dirt is to heat the boiler with gas, either propane or butane LPG. Combined with a tubular flash boiler, this will give almost instantaneous steam and will be perfectly safe provided the cylinders are vented overboard. Then you have a quick, clean method of propulsion. Of course it can be argued that you are still producing unwanted burnt gases, but these are less toxic than those of petrol and diesel, and they are going into the atmosphere rather than direct into possible drinking water supplies. Arguments regarding the greenhouse effect we will leave to weightier tomes than this.

Even with a gas heating system though, steam propulsion will still be an enthusiast's hobby, with the engine and associated tinkering usually being more important to the owner than getting anywhere in particular.

Traditional boats

So far we have looked at alternative power plants; we turn now to traditional boats in general. We use the word traditional rather than vintage or veteran, as age is less important than the style of the craft. In fact many of today's 'traditional' boats are made from glass fibre, using a classic design as the basis of the mould and with the fittings and detail joinery in wood and brass.

A beautifully restored wooden umpire's launch, seen here at Henley.

Thus you have the benefits of modern material, with its ease of construction and maintenance, but with looks that will stand out from the mass of boats on the river.

However, for the true purist only wooden construction will do. By its very nature wood is a material that rots if it is not constantly maintained, and a wooden boat is ideal for the person with time on his hands or the resources to employ someone else to do the work. Old wooden boats are still occasionally found rotting away in backwaters, and several firms have grown up specializing in the restoration of these craft. In many cases virtually the whole of the boat is replaced, leaving only the original shape. The cost of this skilled work is not cheap, with restoration of a medium-sized launch costing anything from £50,000 to £200,000, but the end result is beautiful to behold.

Traditional boats can be from the 1930s, '40s or '50s, and be of a style not dissimilar to today's cruisers. Alternatively they can date from the turn of the century, in which case they will mainly be dayboats. The classic Edwardian river launch has an elegance all of its own, and lucky is the person who owns one. Of a more modern style is the Thames slipper launch, recognizable by its unique sloping aft deck. Made famous by Andrews of Maidenhead in the 1920s and '30s, it was copied by many yards on the river. The petrol engine is mounted under the foredeck, and the boat provides seats for four or six people. The aft deck and the underwater shape were designed to cause a minimum of wash, producing the ideal craft for the river.

Unique amongst wooden cruisers are the boats that in 1940 formed the armada of small craft that helped rescue the British Expeditionary Force from the advancing German armies. Known forever after as the Dunkirk Little Ships, this motley collection of launches, fireboats and tugs braved the English Channel and the *Luftwaffe* to ferry more than 350,000 British and French troops from the Normandy beaches out to the waiting warships. Some were lost in the action, but many survived and have now become collectors' items. They have been lovingly restored and maintained by their owners who hold regular rallies to commemorate the event.

Other traditional boats include electric canoes, popular at the beginning of the century, and electric punts. Add to these 'umpire's' launches, converted working boats such as inspectors' launches, police launches, fireboats and tugs, and you have a wide selection of different types still afloat.

Of course a traditional boat does not have to be only a river craft. Many sea-going vessels survive and have been restored, but the ravages of salt water and the action of waves and tides take a greater toll than the muddy waters of rivers and lakes. Also, the safety standards that have to apply to a vessel going to sea are harder to achieve with older craft, making them more expensive to restore and maintain.

7

Mediterranean boating

An increasing number of people now go boating in the Med. Even taking into account the recent spate of good summers in Britain, the attractions of the Mediterranean are obvious: guaranteed sunshine, no tides, and a surplus of beaches, islands and coves. Even the distance is not so much of a problem. It can be as quick to get from London to Nice as it is to drive to Lymington from London on a Friday evening.

But surely it is expensive, you ask? Well, the answer is that it is not as expensive as you would think, and if your leisure time is precious the benefits will offset this. Alternatively, if you have a trailable boat you can tow it to the Med for a holiday and reduce the cost of boating there even more.

What boat should you buy?

The Mediterranean has bred its own particular style of boat. The accent is on open cockpits, with plenty of room for sunbathing and taking the air. Add to this a large bathing platform, with a good ladder to get back on board after your swim. The sun can be fierce, so some sort of shade is essential – Americans call them Bimini tops, but whatever, a quickly erected canvas hood is vital. Similarly, light colours for gel-coat and upholstery are best, as they reflect rather than absorb the heat.

Catering on board is often limited to an icebox or fridge, to keep drinks and food cool. The fridge must be large enough and have sufficient power to cool down quickly, otherwise it will be of no use. A back-up icebox is useful if you have an extra large party. Alternatively, a 12V ice-maker rapidly earns its keep.

Pressurized cold water is normally installed for drinking and for washing off on the bathing platform after a swim. The

Mediterranean is salty, and the dried crystals can rapidly intensify the sun to burn the skin.

Of course, some boats run to full cooking facilities, with air-conditioning as an added luxury, but the above items are the minimum essentials. An efficient anchoring system is also vital, preferably with an electric winch that can be operated from the helm as well as from the foredeck. Berthing in Mediterranean marinas is usually done stern first, and while there may sometimes be a buoy to tie the bow to, you often have to drop your own anchor and then pay out the chain as you approach the quay astern. The anchor also allows you to lie off a beach and enjoy the surroundings, while keeping clear of the crush.

Twin engines are the most popular option; the Med has an exposed coastline, so the second engine is an important safety factor. Petrol is preferred to diesel for boats up to 30ft, and often for craft larger than this. The UK's favourable tax incentive for diesel fuel does not apply to nearly the same degree in Europe, with diesel being around 75 to 80 per cent of the price of petrol. The relatively lighter use of the boat means that you will rarely use enough fuel to make up the higher extra cost of the diesel engine in fuel savings. Make sure that the engine is one that can be serviced locally where you plan to keep the boat. There is

The ultimate fun in the sun – a Sunseeker 24 off the French Côte d'Azur.

nothing more time consuming and frustrating than organizing repairs at a distance in a foreign country. This, of course, applies to any major items of equipment you have fitted – check with the maker whether they have local agents.

If you want to travel any distance a seaworthy hull is essential. Don't be deluded by the picture postcards – the Mediterranean can produce vicious seas with short steep waves very rapidly, making a deep-vee hull the only choice if you want to carry on travelling fast or even moderately fast. However, if beach-hopping and travelling no further than the nearest cove is all you want to do then the simplest of craft, an outboard-powered inflatable, will be perfect for your needs.

The popularity of the Mediterranean market has meant that many companies now build boats aimed at its particular requirements. Thus you no longer have to buy an Italian or French boat in order to have one suitable for the Med. In the UK this trend was led by Sunseeker, with their range of fast open-cockpit sports cruisers, but now nearly all the major manufacturers have models suitable for a life in the sun. The Scandinavians have also surprisingly latched onto the market, with Swedish and Norwegian designs being prominent, while the giant American companies are also turning their sights to this lucrative region.

Where to buy your boat

The next question is whether you should buy your boat in the UK or in the country where it is to be kept. The answer is that there are advantages to both.

If you are a permanent UK resident and you buy a boat in the UK which is immediately exported, you are not liable to British VAT. If you then only keep the boat in commission overseas for a maximum of six months of the year, you should avoid paying VAT in the country where it is kept. This is the present case, but the situation can change from day-to-day so it is well to check carefully at the time you are contemplating buying a boat. In practice, you comply with the 'out of commission' period by lodging the ship's papers with the local customs or harbour authorities. How the situation will alter when 1992 arrives is still not clear at the time of writing.

The drawback to this method of purchase is that the dealer you buy from will be based in the UK, and in theory it will not be easy to arrange for after-sales service or warranty work to be done. In practice, however, most British companies have arrangements in Mediterranean countries to cover this, but you should check carefully before you buy. Also you will have the expense of transporting the boat to the Med. A plus factor, of course, is that you can buy in British currency, and you can easily test the boat before you decide on your purchase.

If you buy your boat from an overseas dealer and he completes the paperwork correctly, it should still be possible to avoid liability for British VAT, but this is more complex and you should check first with both the dealer and the British Customs and Excise. The obvious benefit of buying abroad is, of course, ease of access to the dealer should the boat develop a fault. The dealer may also be able to organise a berth for you, which can often be a problem in the Med, and he can look after the boat in your absence and service it at the end of the season.

Gardiennage

With your boat spending most of its life 600 miles or so away from you, looking after it by remote control brings its own problems. The solution adopted by many people is known as *gardiennage*. Individuals in the port will keep an eye on your boat for a set fee. The amount they charge and what you get for your money will of course vary from simply checking the mooring lines to dealing with all the routine servicing and maintenance. Of course the reliability of these so-called *capitans* will also vary, which is where the local knowledge of the dealer could be to your benefit.

The major servicing work is usually carried out by companies in the marina, who are sometimes the dealers themselves. The boat will be taken away to dry storage for the winter, the engines and mechanics will be checked and serviced, and the interior and exterior valeted. Often the routine work will be carried out at fixed prices, with repairs quoted as extras.

In some cases servicing companies have taken over the whole business of storing and looking after boats, with craft not having a set berth in the marina. Instead they are stored undercover for eleven months of the year, only being launched for the owner's annual holiday. The advantages of this system are reduced wear and deterioration in the water and no annual berth to find and pay for. The storage areas, being away from the prime water-front sites, are cheaper and more readily available.

Which country?

For many years the choice of location was either France or Italy. The tourist structure was well organized in these countries, and marinas had grown up rapidly. Gradually the marinas filled and the costs rose, so people started looking further afield. This move was accelerated by political decisions in these two countries in the 1970s to tax foreigners who left their boats behind, and some overall high luxury-goods taxes. These decisions have since been reversed, but the search for other locations continued.

Spain was the first choice, both the mainland and the Balearic Islands of Mallorca, Menorca, Ibiza and Formentera. The popularity of these locations was helped by low prices and the availability of cheap charter flights. As a result, marinas sprang up overnight, though often with very few facilities and little in the way of attractions either inside or out in the surrounding country. These shortcomings are gradually being improved, but it is worth checking before you make your decision. At the end of the day, the attractiveness of the French Côte d'Azur and the Italian Riviera cannot be disputed and will continue to guarantee their popularity whatever the cost.

Other destinations include Greece, Turkey and even Tunisia, but despite the marina-building programmes the distance of these countries from Northern Europe starts to tell against them, and the lack of facilities for servicing and maintaining modern boats can become a problem.

Getting your boat to the Med

Assuming you have bought your boat in the UK, your first concern is to get it to the Mediterranean. Three options are available: overland by road, through the French canals or round by sea.

Trucking the boat by road is probably the preferred option, certainly for vessels up to 40ft long. The risk of damage is reduced, the time it will take is predictable, and it does not tie up any of your own time. Several companies specialize in this business, and the dealer you buy from will be happy to advise. They may even have their own operation if they are a large enough concern. On the other hand, this is likely to be the most expensive method of transporting your boat, and it means you miss the chance of what is for many people a once in a lifetime opportunity.

The next option is taking the boat across the English Channel

The simplest and most reliable way to get your boat to the Med is by road.
(*Photo*: Patrick Kelley)

*Travel through the canals and you will see a France that even the French
don't know – here a hire boat slips along the Burgundy Canal.*

and through the French canals. You can either make the trip yourself and take the opportunity of seeing a very special side of France, or pay a crew to do it for you. Limiting dimensions for the boat are a 1.8m (5ft 10in) draught, and most important, a 3.5m (11ft 6in) air draught – the height of the boat above the water, which governs whether you can pass under the bridges. Specific dimensions of individual canals should be checked in advance, and an allowance made for dry weather, with consequent shallow depths. The trip through the canals can be hard on a boat, as there are several hundred locks to negotiate, so it should be well fendered and wrapped up. The journey is likely to take three weeks at minimum and closer to five if you are taking it at leisure, so it is not an option for busy owners. However, as we have said, it is a unique opportunity to see a side of France that even the French know little about.

The third option is to take the boat round by sea – across the Bay of Biscay and through the Straits of Gibraltar. For most boats longer than 50ft this is the only possibility, while for 40 footers it is an option that can be considered. A boat smaller than this may have an uncomfortable trip. Taking the sea route requires careful planning, as many of today's boats do not have the fuel capacity for long passages. It also requires a fully experienced crew – do not be tempted to do it short-handed. The job can also be done by a professional commercial delivery crew. If you wish to make the journey yourself it is still a good idea to pay an experienced hand to come along and help. If you are lucky the trip can be done in 10 to 14 days, but bad weather can double this. Of course you also have to budget for the boat's fuel, crew costs, and travelling back home at the end.

The final method, which applies to trailable boats only, is to tow it to the Med yourself. The limit for car towability is probably 21ft, though with a Land Rover you could manage up to 24ft or so. This method is a possibility for deliveries of boats that are not coming back, but it is also an option for holiday-only trips. You can have a lot of fun with your own runabout in the Med, perhaps using it for day trips only and staying in a campsite at night. Be prepared for a long haul down, though. From northern France to the Med is the best part of 600 miles whichever way you look at it, and French roads at holiday times can be agony. Plan to do the journey in two stages, allowing yourself an overnight stop en route.

Rules and regulations

Whether you will be leaving your boat permanently in the Med or just trailing it down for a holiday, it is essential that all your documentation is in order. Boating might be unfettered by regulations in the UK, but this is not so abroad.

To start with, the boat must be registered. This can either be via the Small Ships Register for privately-owned craft up to 24m (79ft), or better still with full British Registration. Proof of this registration must be carried on board at all times, and this means the original documents not copies. Details of registration are covered in Chapter 10.

A proper bill of sale is also needed. Many second-hand boats change owners with just a cheque and a handshake, and never have such a document. If you are intending to go abroad make sure you get a bill of sale, such as that provided by the Royal Yachting Association (RYA), when you buy the boat.

Insurance is also essential, particularly with adequate third party cover, should you injure someone else. The skipper and anyone else intending to drive the boat must have proof of their competence to do so. An RYA certificate is the best way to achieve this (see Chapter 10). If you have taken the requisite courses you will be awarded the appropriate document. If you have not, then it is possible to obtain an RYA Helmsman's Certificate of Competence via a club or similar body. In any case, the RYA will advise on the particular requirements of the country you will be visiting.

If you are towing a boat abroad for a holiday it is important to have documentation covering boat, trailer and engine. This should be in the form of registration and bill of sale for the boat, plus invoices for engine and trailer. To save problems, these should be declared to customs on your way out of England and into France. Again, proof of insurance cover and a helmsman's certificate should be included.

Weather

It might seem a little strange to talk about bad weather in a chapter on the Mediterranean. After all, this is what you are going there to avoid. Do not be deceived. Whilst conditions in the summer are usually beautiful, they can change rapidly. The Mediterranean is surrounded by huge land masses with potentially vast differences in temperature. From the chilly Alps to the north, to the baking Sahara in the south, the huge temperature variations can cause fierce winds to blow. So sudden and severe can these winds be that they have been given their own names by the locals. The evocative-sounding sirocco, mistral and tramontana are in reality potentially serious winds. On land they can cause damage to property and crops. Out at sea they can build up short, steep seas in less than an hour, and catch out the unprepared boat. Even on a good day, the sea breeze, caused by the land heating up faster than the water, will bring a short, sharp chop to the water during the middle of the afternoon that will die away in the evening as fast as it came.

All this is simply to warn you that you must watch the weather if you are going on anything but the shortest of trips. Pay attention to forecasts, and if in doubt ask at the marina office. If predicted conditions do not look good, spend the day on the beach or take time to visit the surrounding countryside. Then when the forecast is better really go out and enjoy the sun.

——— 8 ———
Building
your own boat

For many would-be sailors, the only way of acquiring the boat of their dreams is to build it, or fit it out themselves. An advantage of this method is reduced cost, plus the fact that you can choose the layout and design exactly to suit yourself. The disadvantage is the time it takes to complete the project. Be realistic about this, and do not undertake a vessel that is too large. The front gardens of Britain are littered with the mouldering dreams of over-ambitious boatbuilders.

A realistic maximum size for most individuals to tackle is 30ft. Beyond this you will need an army of helpers or an enthusiasm that most people cannot muster. Of course, if you are fitting-out a canal narrowboat these guidelines are influenced by the reduced accommodation for shorter lengths and the relative simplicity of the interiors, but even here 45ft is the biggest project that most people should undertake.

Material

In the earliest days of home boat building the plywood construction of most craft enabled the amateur builder to tackle the hull as well as the interior. There are still plans available for home construction in plywood but the advent of glass fibre has largely superseded wood for the hull. The cost and complication of building a plug and mould are uneconomic for individuals to tackle themselves, so as a result most people start with the hull ready-made in GRP. There are methods available for home construction in GRP using foam sandwich or glass rods for a frame, but again, these are unusual and time consuming.

Another hull material commonly employed is steel. Again, the equipment and facilities required for steel fabrication and welding are usually beyond the amateur, so a ready-built hull is the normal starting point. The exception to this is the De Groot range of steel boats from Holland, for which you are supplied with a complete kit of precut steel plates and sections which just require welding together to make the hull.

As a general rule, GRP is chosen for fast boats as it is lighter than steel. It is also easier for the amateur to work with, as the bonding-in of components is a simpler technique to learn than welding and requires no costly equipment.

For canal narrowboats a different set of rules applies. Their box shape is simpler and stronger to build in steel, and the material better withstands the rough treatment the boats will receive in locks. Provided you specify in advance where you want bearers and frames for equipment etc. to be welded in by the builder, there should be no need for you to do any welding.

Choosing the right hull

As with all other aspects of your boating, the correct choice of hull depends on where you plan to do most of your cruising: on rivers, canals or the sea. Check who the designer is and ask what other craft he has produced for similar applications. If possible ask to see examples of similar boats already built – this should not be difficult, and the builder should at least be able to show you photographs.

Checking the standard of construction of the hull you have ordered is the next problem. With a steel hull you can specify the thickness of the material you require, and be able reasonably simply to check that it has been used. You should also look at the welds and the fairness or smoothness of the plating.

With glass fibre the problem is not so straightforward. Once the layers of glass have been laminated together it is not possible to tell how many were used. In this case you should ask to see the lay-up schedule. Ask what the finished weight of the hull should be, and if possible check that this has been adhered to. This can be done either by the crane driver, or by weighing trailer or transporter and boat on a commercial weighbridge, and then weighing the transporter only. Finally, if any cut-outs have been made in the hull for outdrive motors, portholes, skinfittings, etc. ask that these be retained for inspection. Their thickness can give an indication of the weight of glass that has been employed at that point, though this will not tell you what has happened elsewhere.

For larger vessels, the company may offer you a Lloyd's Hull

Release Note. This is issued by Lloyd's Register, and shows that the hull has been made in accordance with standards and weights laid down at the design stage. This service will cost you a fee, but it is well worth it with larger craft for peace of mind and to improve the resale value of the boat once it is finished.

In all cases, if you are in any doubt as to your experience or ability to check these matters, employ a qualified surveyor to do the job for you. It will be money well spent in the long run. Also it perhaps goes without saying that buying from a long-standing, reputable firm is your best bet.

Choosing the building area

Part of the decision on which hull you are going to buy must be governed by the space you have to build it in. Remember to allow enough room to get round it on all sides, as well as underneath. Remember that the finished boat will be taller than when you began with cabin, superstructure, mast and so on, and deeper, with stern gear, propellers and rudders. Remember that a rudder will need clearance underneath to fit it in place. This can be achieved by digging a hole, but not if you have set the boat up on a concrete base.

The finished boat will also be considerably heavier than the bare hull. If it has to be craned into or out of the building site you will incur extra costs. The size of the crane that has to be employed is governed not only by the weight of the boat but by its distance away from the nearest point of access. This can multiply the size of crane and hence its cost considerably, and it should be checked before making your plans.

Obviously it is more convenient if the boat can be built as near as possible to your home. Time is not wasted travelling or on return journeys for forgotten pieces of equipment. The front garden is the favoured choice for most builders, but check that this location does not infringe any local planning regulations or by-laws. It is also sensible and courteous to tell your neighbours what you intend to do.

If building at home is not feasible the next best alternative is a nearby boatyard. The advantages here are that facilities for lifting and moving both the hull and the finished boat are on site. Items of equipment that you might require during the construction are also close to hand, as is frequently some helpful advice. It is also easy to take a quick peek at someone else's boat if you are stuck on any particular point.

Preparing the building area

Well before the hull arrives you should prepare the ground. This should be as level as possible, with solid timbers arranged to take the weight of the boat. The favourite choice for these are railway sleepers which are well seasoned and large enough to spread the load. These will take the main weight under the keel. To prevent the boat falling over you need side supports under the bilge or chines. These should be stable enough to withstand any rocking in high winds. The supports should also have a base large enough to spread the load and prevent them digging into soft ground. Oil drums serve this purpose admirably. Alternatively, wooden struts can be used, but they must be thick enough not to flex. They must also be secured, preferably to one another, to prevent them slipping out. Take care to spread the load of keel and chine supports evenly, with wooden pads between them and the hull to stop localized distortion or cracking.

Setting up the boat

When the hull arrives it is essential that it is set up level. Every angle inside the finished boat depends on the correct fore-and-aft and athwartships alignment. The hull should arrive with a level waterline marked on it to enable this to be done more easily, but you should check this in advance with the builder. Levelling the boat while the crane is there is easy. Once it has gone you will have serious problems.

Check the hull all over for any damage or flaws. These may have been caused during either the construction or transport – but now is the time to find out and take it up with the companies concerned.

Once the boat is set up you should decide whether you want it covered or not. If you are building through the winter, which is likely, a cover will keep off the worst of the weather. It will also help in keeping you and the boat warm. The best choice is clear plastic, as it lets the light through, but make sure that it is well secured and protected from chafing. There is nothing more annoying than flapping plastic, which will also rapidly tear.

An electricity line is a must, but be sure that it is of large diameter to take the current over the distance, especially since you will probably be running a heater off it. Also, ensure that you have an Earth Leakage Circuit-Breaker fitted where the line is taken from the house supply, otherwise damage to the line, or damp, will be potentially fatal.

Fitting out

It is not our intention here to go into the detail of fitting out, but a few points are worth noting.

First, be quite clear which parts of the job you are qualified to tackle. The others you will do well to give to a professional.

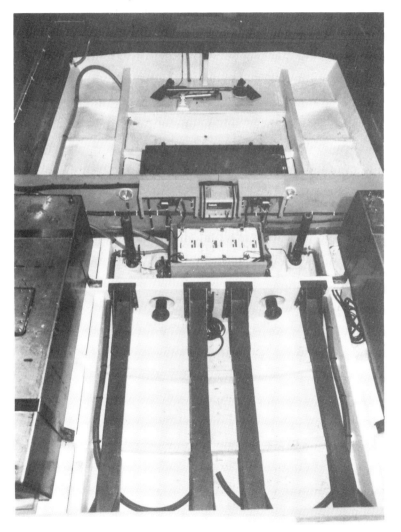

A Colvic 43 with engine-bearers and sterngear ready installed.

Under the latter heading will often be electric fittings and the engine installation. Getting these right is critical to the project, and it is important that they are done properly. Some hull manufacturers will also fit the engine and associated components, which will save you a lot of time and effort and will ensure they are done correctly.

Secondly, many expensive items of equipment and gear can be bought at discounts at the many boat jumble sales and shows around the country. Make a list at the beginning of the project of everything you will need, together with prices, and take it with you to the shows. Even if you do not want all the items at the early stage of construction, buying them cheaply will save you money in the long run. Beware, though, that you may not get a guarantee with goods bought in this way, or it may be out of date by the time you actually come to fit the item in the boat.

Whether to buy or hire tools is another key question. Some items you will need to use continuously through the project, and these should be bought. Other occasional-use tools are often better hired when you need them. When buying tools do not choose the cheapest DIY models. Typical examples of this are an electric drill and a jigsaw. Continuous use on fibre glass and wood will quickly wear out low-power versions, so you are best advised to go for semi-professional models.

Motoraway boats

One of the longest established hull moulding companies, Colvic, have recently introduced a concept called the Motoraway boat. With this scheme you buy a boat that, as its name implies, is completed to a stage where you could actually launch it and drive away. Thus it has the engines fitted, sterngear, propellers and rudders, fuel tanks and lines, batteries and electrical system, throttles and gear controls at both the inside helm and flying bridge positions, plus all the stainless steel work such as guard-rails and cleats. Windows are also fitted in toughened glass and aluminium frames, as are the navigation lights. All that is left for you to do is the joinery, upholstery and fitting out.

The range is aimed mainly at small boatyards, which are unable to manufacture all these items themselves, or at private owners wishing to employ sub-contract labour to do the fitting out. However, it would provide the perfect way for an amateur boat-builder to take on a larger craft than he would otherwise be able to tackle. Models in the range go from 29ft up to 43ft at present, with a 53 footer soon to go into production.

9

Buying: new
or second-hand?

Now that you have decided which type of boat you want, the next
question is do you buy new or second-hand? Don't be put off by
the connotation of the term second-hand. On average, twice as
many people start with a used boat as a new one, and many
never own a new boat in their lives. It is a perfectly acceptable
route to go – after all the house you live in was almost certainly
not new when you bought it, and the same thinking applies to
boats.

The reluctance to buy a used boat usually arises from our
experiences with that other major item of capital purchase, the
car. This has a finite lifespan and deteriorates rapidly towards
the end of it. A boat on the other hand, if well maintained, will
remain strong and reliable for many years. Often subsequent
owners will add extras and equipment that will actually increase
the boat's value, and you can be sure that all the new boat bugs
will have been ironed out. It will also be fully equipped, often
with everything you need for cruising, including pots and pans,
crockery, ropes, fenders, boathook, and all the gear that you
would otherwise have to buy. A second-hand boat also has the
advantage that it is immediately available, whereas you will
have to await delivery of a new vessel for sometimes months or
even a year for the most popular models.

Second-hand

When looking for a second-hand boat there are two main
sources: brokers or classified advertisements. Brokers have a
similar function to estate agents in that they do not normally
own the boats they have for sale; they instead act as agents for
the owner. They advertise lists of boats in magazines and will

often have their offices in marinas. The boats will frequently be moored in or near that marina, but this is not always the case. As with houses, the same boat can sometimes be found on more than one broker's list.

In practice, a broker does operate in a way similar to an estate agent. He takes particulars of a boat from the owner and passes them on to prospective buyers. He will show potential purchasers around the boat and, if required, take them on demonstration trips. He will take and hold a deposit and will deal with the other aspects of the sale, including drawing up a bill of sale and receiving the money from the customer. For this he charges a commission of 8 to 10 per cent to the seller.

It is important that the buyer be aware of the relationship between the broker and the seller, because while the broker does his best to ensure that the particulars stated about a boat are correct, he gives no guarantee of their accuracy. Typical areas where problems can arise concern the age of the boat, the number of hours on its engines, its history of ownership, and even its speed. The seller may claim that it is a 1985 model capable of 20 knots, whereas in reality it may be a 1980 boat that has never done more than 15 knots in its life. Thus it is vital for the buyer to make his own independent assessment of a boat.

Surveys

As with house purchases the recommended route when buying a boat is to employ a qualified surveyor. For an agreed fee he will give a condition report on a craft you are considering. Charges vary according to the size of the boat and how detailed the survey is. Currently one typical formula for a purchase survey is:

Survey fee in £ = Length of boat × Beam (in feet) ÷ 1.0 or 1.2

To this must be added the surveyor's travelling allowance, plus VAT. Thus a typical 30ft boat will cost in the region of £250–£300 to survey plus travel and VAT.

For this the surveyor will report on all visible aspects of the boat. He will not normally report on the engines, except on their external appearance, and he will not report on the hull unless the boat is already out of the water or you pay to have it lifted out. Nor will he report on performance and speed unless you request a sea trial.

From this you can see that a survey is not cheap, so you should use it more as a means of confirming your own judgement about a boat than as a first step in the process. The survey should stop you from buying a bad boat or allow you to negotiate a lower price for a boat that has problems, but the first assessment should be made by you.

Making your own assessment

So how do you go about making this first assessment of a potential purchase? As in other matters, if you are unsure of your own qualifications it helps if you can take along a knowledgeable friend. If not, these steps may help.

Walk around the inside and outside of the boat on your own, without the broker, taking notes on what you see. Look for obvious signs of damage – scratches and gouges in the gel-coat, chips in the paint etc. A few of these are inevitable in any boat, but they should have been repaired. The repairs will never be completely invisible, but the better they are, the more likely they are to have been carried out by a professional rather than botched by the owner. On the outside of the boat prime spots for damage are the corners of the transom, the chines, the stem, and the underwater hull, especially sprayrails on a fast boat. Look for crazing (small cracks) and cracks in the gel-coat of the

Check the propeller, shaft and rudder for corrosion and wear.

topsides, especially around amidships and up by the gunwales, where it may have been banged when coming alongside.

If the boat is out of the water check the condition of the underwater gear – propellers, rudders, shafts etc. Propellers should be smooth around the edges of the blades; signs to look out for are chips in the edges – again a few small ones are acceptable. None of the blades should be bent. Check one blade against another to see if they match. A propeller can be repaired, but it will cost you money, and the extent of the damage is indicative of how well the boat has been driven and looked after.

Shafts and rudders run in bearings, and these can wear out. Put your weight against prop or rudder and see how much it moves. Some slack is inevitable, but looseness or rattling will be expensive to fix. If you are not sure what is good or bad in this area, take a quick peek under the newest nearby boat for comparison. The anodes should also be checked. These are silver blocks of zinc bolted to the hull near the sterngear. Their purpose is to reduce electrolytic corrosion of the underwater equipment, and they do this by corroding away themselves. Thus if an anode is working correctly it should be approximately 25–50 per cent wasted away after a year. More than this in a year indicates a problem. Less than this, and they are not doing their job. A correctly wasted surface is pitted.

If the anodes have not been working correctly the sterngear itself could be starting to corrode. At first this will not be immediately evident but there are two ways of checking. One is to tap the rudder or prop with a coin. If it is in good condition, it will ring like a bell. If it is corroded, it will give a dull clunk. Again, practice on a nearby new boat to get your ear correctly tuned! The second method is to scratch the surface, again with a coin. If the material exposed is good it will be a yellowy brass colour. If it is bad it will be pink, showing that the zinc in the bronze alloy has dissolved, leaving only the weak copper.

On deck, check the condition of ropes, fenders and covers. Check how secure the guard-rails and stanchions are by leaning against them and seeing if they move. Check the cleats and then the gel-coat around the bases of these fittings for damage or cracks. Check also the anchor and chain for corrosion.

Inside the boat, the most important problems to look for are leaks and damp. Leaks will usually come from windows, hatches and door. Feel underneath these for wet patches. If it has not been raining recently these may have dried, but the telltale evidence is discolouration beneath them or streaks on the upholstery or bulkheads. Sealing windows can be an expensive

problem. General damp will be indicated by a musty smell inside
the boat or in lockers, with discolouration or actual mould on
woodwork and upholstery. It is usually caused by poor ventilation, and while the cause can be cured the results may be
expensive to put right. Obviously, you should also look under the
floorboards for leaks through the hull. If he has any sense the
seller will have pumped the resulting water out before you
arrive, but the giveaway evidence is tidemarks around the side
of the boat at different levels.

A general inspection of the interior should include a look for
overall wear-and-tear on all the upholstery and furniture, as
well as a running check of all the equipment, lights etc. Take
along a camera and shoot a roll of film as you go. It will help
refresh your memory when you get home. It will also remind you
to ask what equipment is included in the sale price. Items have a
habit of disappearing between the agreement to sell and the
final handing over.

The engine should obviously be a priority on your list, and
even if you are not a qualified mechanic there is much that you
can tell using common sense. Check the oil and water – low
levels indicate a sloppy owner. Check for oil leaks on the engine
and underneath. Look at the batteries too – an expensive item
on any boat, if they have not been well maintained they will give
you endless trouble. If they are lost under a heap of junk they
will probably not have been looked after. Check the cleanliness
of the terminals and the electrolyte levels. Check all round the
engine compartment for rust, oil and dirt. Ask what the engine
hours are. On average a pleasure boat will do between 50 and
200 hours per season, with 100 being a good average. A
well-maintained marine diesel engine will run at least 1,000
hours, often as many as 2,000, without any overhauls, though if
they are poorly serviced they can be giving problems at half this
life.

Overall, you are looking for a boat that has been cared for and
maintained. Ask for any documentation of the vessel's past life:
service history of the engines, invoices for annual maintainance
and repair, a log book for running information etc. A well-looked
after craft will have all of these; absence should put you on your
guard. Boats suffer more from neglect and lack of use than from
continual running.

If you are getting close to a decision, it is important to take the
boat out for a trial. Not only will this tell you something about
how it handles, it will also confirm the top speed and give you
valuable insight into the condition of the engines. Do not trust

the speedometer (log) as they are notorious for being optimistic, sometimes in error of up to 4–5 knots over true speed on planing boats. Instead, look for a measured distance to check against. If you are not confident in your ability to do this, ask the surveyor to carry it out. Regarding the machinery, find out the manufacturer's quoted maximum rpm for the particular engine model fitted, then check these underway. They should be within 200rpm or better, and both engines in a twin installation should be within 100rpm of each other. In this respect, rev counters are usually more reliable than speedometers, but not always so. Make sure you run the engines underway at full speed for at least 15 minutes, and check the gauges during this time. Problems with overheating or low oil pressure will often not show up in a quick five-minute burst of speed.

As we have said the surveyor will give you a general report on the engines, but if you want more information it is often good value to ask the local dealer for the particular make to come down to the boat and produce a report for you. It is usually money well spent.

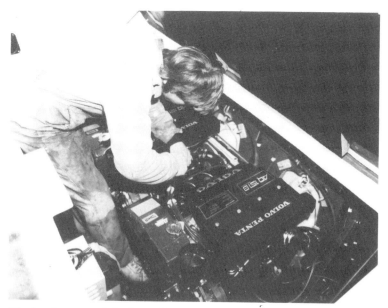

The local approved dealer will give you a report on the engines. Here a mechanic checks a pair of Volvo 151hp petrol stern-drive motors.

Once you have made up your mind that you have found the right boat you can call in your surveyor. Depending on what his report says you then make an offer through the broker for the boat. If the survey highlights major problems you can use these to negotiate a lower price, but bear in mind that every second-hand boat can be expected to have some problems, and these may already be reflected in the asking price.

If your offer is accepted you will be expected to make a deposit, usually 10 per cent, while other formalities are put in motion. These include checking to see that the vendor is actually the legal owner of the boat and finding out if there are any mortgage or finance charges on the vessel. If a marine mortgage has been taken out on the boat it will have been required to be registered, and the charge will be noted on the register. However, cases have come to light in which a boat has been sold once with a finance charge undeclared, and subsequently resold with the new owner being unaware of the charge. There is currently no hard-and-fast answer to this problem, though thankfully it is extremely rare and the risk is reduced if evidence of all the previous changes of ownership is available.

In this respect it should be stated that the Small Ships Register, described in Chapter 10, does not itself give final proof of ownership. A boat can be stolen, then subsequently reregistered under a different name. Again there is no ultimate answer, except to request all previous bills of sale, plus supporting documentation such as marina bills, service invoices, and insurance documents. A thief will, of course, have none of these.

Buying privately

So far we have assumed you are buying your second-hand boat through a broker. You can of course buy privately, usually through classified advertisements. The main source of these are the monthly motorboating magazines, *Exchange and Mart*, and your local paper. A paper from a coastal town is likely to have more boats listed than one away from the water. The procedure is much the same as with a broker – make your own first assessment, then call in a surveyor. In this case though, you will have to draw up your own bill of sale; the RYA have a suitable standard one that you can buy.

One other source of private sales is the noticeboards of clubs – another good reason for joining one.

Buying through specialist dealers

A recent development has been dealers in new boats who buy or take in part-exchange second-hand models of the make they specialize in. They then service these, check them over, and offer them for sale with usually a short-term warranty. In this case you are buying from the dealer, who takes on the responsibility of ensuring the condition of the boat and the accuracy of its particulars. Prices will usually be higher than buying privately, but you will have more assurance about what you are purchasing.

Prices

This brings us to the hardest question of all to answer: What is the value of a second-hand boat? Unfortunately, unlike for cars, there is no *Glass's Guide* to base figures upon. It has been tried in the past, but the small numbers of each model on the market at any given time make estimates impossible. Also the condition between one boat and the next varies considerably and different amounts of equipment on board greatly affect prices. The only answer is to check the advertisements for similar boats and compare prices. Seasonally you can expect to pay the most between March and June, with the lowest prices at the end of the year.

Buying new

New boats will usually be bought from a dealer, or sometimes straight from the manufacturer. The best place to make your first inspection is at a boat show, as you will find the greatest number of models and makes on display. The principal UK shows are in London in January and in Southampton in September. These are followed by the regional shows: Glasgow and Birmingham in February, Bristol in April, and Ipswich in May.

Do not make your final decision at a show though. Arrange a demonstration run so that you can see the boat in its natural environment and can better appreciate its good and bad points. Try to take it out in conditions similar to those in which you plan to use it, and take the whole family along with you.

It may sound strange to say so, but it is often worth having a surveyor inspect your boat during the course of its construction, particularly if it is an expensive model. Brief him on how you intend to use it, and he will keep you informed on progress and offer valuable advice on the suitability of some of the equipment being fitted.

Delivery is one of the most vexing subjects concerning the purchase of new boats. Some builders are notoriously optimistic or inaccurate in their delivery schedules, and it is not unknown to hear stories of boats ordered at the London Boat Show in January with a promised delivery date of May, eventually arriving in September when the whole season has finished. Excuses range from production problems, excessive demand, to sick employees, but the end result is anguish for the owner who has usually booked and paid for a marina berth, arranged holidays, and perhaps sold his existing boat.

Again it is hard to be specific with advice in this area. Join a boat club and ask around for people's experiences with different makes. Ask the manufacturer how many boats of a particular model have been built and what the rate of production is – new models tend to have more problems than established lines. Boats up to 20ft you can expect to be coming off the line of a UK builder at a rate of around 1 per week. 20–30 footers are produced at the

Boat shows are the best place to look at all the models available.

rate of around 2 boats per month, while over 30ft it can vary between 1–2 boats per month. Of course, if you go to a US manufacturer the figure can be 10 times this or more, but only 5–10 per cent are exported usually.

One problem with new models can be the vagueness of the purchase order. Often this is just a simple invoice or order, with no terms or conditions attached to it and no agreement as to what action will result from a failure to meet the stated delivery date. One solution is to use the Contract for the Purchase of a New Boat, available from the RYA or British Marine Industries Federation (BMIF), which can have agreed penalty clauses built into it and is a much more binding document.

Finance

Buying a boat these days can involve anything from signing a credit card slip to a major financial transaction, second in size and complexity only to the purchase of a house. Depending on your aspirations and status, newcomers to boating have the two obvious choices of drawing on existing assets or borrowing money from a wide range of sources to fund the purchase.

In either case, do not over-stretch your resources. Calculate how much the boat will cost per annum, including the loan repayments. Standing charges – insurance, mooring fees and annual maintenance – cannot be avoided, irrespective of the amount of use the boat receives.

If you have to borrow some or all of the purchase price there are three usual routes: you can pay a visit to your bank manager and extend your overdraft or take out a personal loan, you can extend your house mortgage or borrow more than you require when you move, or you can borrow from one of a small number of institutions who deal specifically with marine finance. These latter are usually separate departments of finance houses which are in turn connected to the big banks. Broadly speaking, the finance they will offer you falls into three bands.

1. Unsecured loans with a fixed rate of interest on amounts up to £5,000.
2. Unsecured personal loans with a variable interest rate on amounts up to £15,000.
3. Variable interest rate marine mortgages secured on the boat for amounts over £15,000.

As a rule of thumb, the maximum term of the loan is one year for every £1,000 borrowed with a maximum term of 10 years, but these and all matters concerned with credit can change rapidly. Interest rates vary considerably and are influenced, apart from the base lending rate, by your status, the type of loan (secured loans offer a better risk and usually a lower rate) and the boat you are buying. A survey may be requested, and you may have to register the boat. When comparing like to like, always ask for the APR (annual percentage rate) to make a precise judgement.

Rules and regulations, training, licences and registration

Boating in the UK is still one of the last unregulated pastimes. Newcomers to the sport are often surprised to find that you need neither driving licence nor insurance, but there are some rules, and where they do not exist common sense tells you to make your own provisions to ensure the safety of your boat and its passengers.

Boat licences

Sea-going vessels

If you use your boat only on the sea and do not leave UK waters it does not normally have to be licensed or registered. However, if there is a marine mortgage on it you will have to register it as a British Registered Ship. The Registrar of Shipping is administered by HM Customs and Excise, and your local customs office will give you the address of the nearest registration department. Registration will cost in the region of £180 plus a fee for a surveyor, currently around £100. The surveyor is needed to verify the registered tonnage of the boat, part of the requirements of registration. This 'tonnage' is in fact unrelated to the weight of the boat, being instead a measure of its internal volume. This dates back to the time when a cargo vessel's capacity was assessed by the number of tuns, or barrels of wine, it could carry; ton is a derivation of the word tun. This capacity was and still is used to calculate the light dues and other charges made on a commercial vessel when it visits a port. While charges will not usually be applied to a pleasure boat, the figure is still required.

The boat's registered number and tonnage must then be

carved into a main bulkhead or deck beam, though in deference to the modern materials of today's boats it is permitted to carve the figures on a board which is then fixed permanently to the steel or GRP bulkhead. If you sell a registered boat the Registrar must be notified of the change of ownership, and if you wish to change the boat's name this must be published for a requisite period of time to allow any objections to be made.

From this it can be seen that full registration is a procedure not to be lightly undertaken. However, a simplified form of registration, called the Small Ships Register (SSR) has recently been introduced by the Department of Transport. This can be used by privately owned vessels up to 20m in length and is administered by the RYA. One of its primary purposes is to enable your boat to comply with the requirements of foreign countries. If you take your craft abroad it definitely will need to be registered, and SSR registration is acceptable. The cost at the time of going to press is £10, and the registered number need only be painted or stuck on the side of the boat. Because of the ease with which it can be obtained, the SSR should not be assumed to give proof of ownership of the vessel for the purpose of buying or selling.

Having said all the above, we should point out that proposals have been mooted for several years to introduce compulsory registration of all vessels in the UK. The stated purpose is to raise revenue to pay for the buoys, lights and other navigation aide around the British coast, which are currently paid for entirely by commercial vessels. Opinions on the benefits of compulsory registration vary, particularly since in all other European countries these costs are met through general taxation, and also since it has been suggested that the cost of administering and policing the system would nearly equal the revenue raised. At the time of writing the subject is still in the discussion stages, but compulsory registration might be introduced at any time.

Inland craft

If you use your boat on inland waterways, either temporarily or permanently, it almost certainly will need a licence, and possibly more than one. The revenue generated from these licences goes towards the maintenance of the locks, banks and weirs and the policing of the system. Different authorities are responsible for different stretches of water. The British Waterways Board (BWB) covers most of the narrow and broad canals and some of the canalized rivers. Other rivers used to be under the control of the relevant local water board, but since privatization they have come under the new National Rivers Authority (NRA). Finally, various smaller bodies deal with the remainder of the lakes and rivers in the UK. If you are in any doubt as to the particular authority dealing with a waterway, contact either your local water board or the NRA.

Licence fees vary from one authority to another, but as a guide a 30ft boat could be charged between £110 on the Thames and £180 for the BWB. Unfortunately at the moment, if you travel from one part of the system to another you will need a licence for each. If your visit is a short one a reduced rate is charged, but if you do it regularly two licences will be needed. A scheme may be introduced whereby annual licence holders of one system will be able to obtain reduced rates for others, allowing you to make an extended annual cruise without incurring high cost penalties; this might be in place by the time you read this book.

If you use your boat on the Thames it will have to comply with certain specifications laid down by the authority. These cover all aspects of the boat's construction and equipment, but their primary purpose is to prevent the occurrence of fire on board and to protect the lives of the occupants. The regulations are stringent but sensible, and your craft can be inspected at any time to ensure that it complies. Other authorities have similar specifications, but in the main these are in the form of recommendations rather than regulations. Even so, we strongly suggest that you apply them to your boat. Typical areas covered are fire extinguishers, fuel systems, gas bottles and piping, and ventilation.

Driving licences

In the UK you do not need a licence to drive a boat. However, for your own safety and that of other people on the water we recommend that you undertake some form of training. This can be divided into theoretical and practical.

At its simplest level, boaters on inland waterways can gain theoretical knowledge by reading the various books and magazines on the subject. The individual authorities themselves often provide booklets outlining the by-laws pertaining to their waterways, together with helpful advice on cruising, mooring, and looking after your boat. In addition to these, the Inland Waterways Association publish a cruising guide, as well as a list of books on the subject.

For your practical training on rivers and canals, we recommend that you make your first trips with an experienced boater on board, or join a club and spend a couple of days crewing for another member. It is possible to start off entirely on your own, but you run the risk of unhappy first trips, spoiling the experience for everyone on board. If you have no choice in the matter, then try not to make your first journey with a boat full of people on a busy summer weekend. Take a day off midweek when the waters are far less crowded.

If you are travelling on tidal waters, some sort of formal training is essential. Again this will take a theoretical and a practical form. The Royal Yachting Association administer, a series of courses and certificates with increasing levels of difficulty, suitable for various members of the crew and various areas of cruising. The courses comprise both theoretical and practical sections, and the titles are self-explanatory: Competent Crew, Day Skipper, Coastal Skipper, Yachtmaster Offshore, and Yachtmaster Ocean. Theory can be learnt from correspondence courses, night-school courses, or specialist training schools.

For the practical parts it is usual to go to one of the specialist sea schools. These are approved by the RYA, who will supply you with an up-to-date list. Courses last between one day and a

Training schools will give you instruction from basic theory up to the highest levels on your own or their boats.

week, and can be either on your own boat or on one of the school's boats. You will receive a mixture of theoretical and practical training and undertake various trips. We strongly recommend that both partners participate, as it is vital that you both understand how to operate all aspects of the boat. This not only helps your enjoyment of the sport, but in the event of illness or accident occurring to one of you, the other must be able to take over control of the boat.

Even if you do not have one of the above certificates, if you plan to travel overseas you will require some form of document to prove your competence to a local authority. For this, the RYA provide the Helmsman's Certificate of Competence. To qualify for one of these you must fill in an application form, accompanied by a declaration from an officer of a club or similar body, confirming your experience and ability to handle a boat.

Insurance

As we have already mentioned, insurance for your boat, either comprehensive or third party, is not compulsory if you use it in UK waters only. However, for practical reasons we would stress that you should carry insurance. It should cover both damage and theft to your own boat as well as injury or damage to third

Training is just as important for sports boat owners. This group is learning how to anchor, important in an emergency if the engine should break down.

parties. Rates vary according to the value of the boat, the areas you will be using it in, and your own experience. The speed of the boat is also important – fast boats clearly represent a higher risk than slow, and if you cannot prove your competence or experience you may have difficulty getting cover for high-performance craft. For the smallest dinghy or inflatable you can often obtain sufficient cover by extending your house insurance policy, usually up to a maximum boat value of £2,500, at a typical premium rate of 1.25 per cent. Above this you should go to one of the specialist underwriters or brokers who advertise in the yachting press.

If you take your boat abroad, then insurance will be compulsory, and you must be able to prove you have at least third-party cover, usually for a minimum of £500,000. In this case you should be sure that you take the original policy and certificate with you, not a photocopy.

Radio licences

If you plan to take your boat on the sea we have already recommended that you carry a VHF radio, either portable or fixed. This will ensure that you can keep in contact with other vessels around you, receive navigational or weather warnings and call for help in an emergency. Before you can operate a radio you must have passed an examination set by the Home Office. Upon completion you receive the superbly titled United Kingdom of Great Britain and Northern Ireland Restricted Certificate of Competence in Radio Telephony VHF Only. The restricted amendment is because you are not allowed to operate MF or long-distance radios, for which you have to pass a separate exam.

In practice, the examination is straightforward and can often be sat at a boat show. Otherwise the RYA will send an examiner to your boat club, or you can attend regional sittings. Several books and audio cassettes are available that will give you the necessary information, but if you are still unsure of your abilities you can take a one-day course in the subject.

In the past, the likelihood of your being stopped and checked for your licence has been small, but the increasing congestion of the marine airwaves, often by completely incompetent people, is prompting a greater number of searches. In any case, it is prudent to understand the requirements of VHF use. Marine radio is for safety and navigational purposes only, not for chat, and one day your life may depend on it. It is therefore important that the other crew members on board understand the basics of its operation too, even if they do not all take the exam.

In addition to your operator's licence, the radio on the boat must have its own licence. This ensures that it is manufactured to the right specifications and has been correctly installed. Even a portable hand-held set must be licensed, in this case with a restricted-use certificate.

Collision Regulations

Since we are talking about rules and regulations, this is an appropriate point to mention the basic laws that cover vessels at sea. The International Collision Regulations are the rules of the road that apply to every boat on the water. No matter how small your craft, you must comply with these at all times. They evolved originally for commercial vessels, but you must understand that once you cast off in your own vessel they apply to you. In a restricted waterway you could find yourself in company with ferries, tankers, fishing boats and dredgers, and you have to know how they will behave and what you should do in each situation.

The basic rules cover which side of the channel you should travel on – at sea you drive on the right, the opposite of the UK road system. They also explain which vessel has right of way in different situations, and the sound signals that you can make to indicate what you intend to do. They cover the lights you should carry at night – the correct ones are vital, as they allow other vessels to gauge in which direction you are travelling and how fast. Clearly we cannot cover the regulations in detail here, but there are many books on the subject, and they are covered in all training courses.

Even on rivers you are subject to rules of navigation. These are based on the same principles as their sea-going counterparts, but with modifications to cover the different circumstances raised by currents, bridges, obstructions and locks. Each river will also have its own local by-laws, which will control such matters as speed limits, discharges of bilge-water and sewage, and so on. The onus is on the skipper of a vessel to make sure which regulations are in force for any waters he is travelling in.

Policing

Our final section looks briefly at who enforces the rules of the sea. Unlike on land, the answer to this is complex and responsibility is divided between several bodies.

The weighty matters of collisions between commercial vessels and similar occurrences are the responsibility of the Department of Transport. They issue ship's master's certificates, and can take them away if a master is deemed to have broken the regulations. At the leisure boating level, you are likely to come in contact with either the police or a harbourmaster. The marine police are in fact divisions of the local force and have their own boats. Thus the Hampshire Police control the waters off the coast of that county, the Metropolitan Police control the tidal Thames, and so on. The police will enforce regulations, though the actual prosecution may be carried out by the local authority or the Department of Transport. Within defined areas around a port or harbour the local harbourmaster will have jurisdiction. He can set local by-laws, particularly those regarding speed limits, which will be enforced either by the harbourmaster himself in his launch or by the police. He will also have a specific radio channel on which he controls movements of ships in his area, and you should listen to this, or call him up for navigational information.

On the rivers, you will encounter police launches, again part of the local force, plus inspectors' launches from the NRA. Both can enforce the by-laws of the waterway.

If all this talk of rules and police has in any way put you off getting afloat, don't be afraid. Boating is still all about relaxation and pleasure. There is no better way to unwind from today's pressures, and providing you follow the guidelines laid down in this book, you will be starting out on the right foot.

As you progress further the other books in this Adlard Coles *Motorboats Monthly* series will give you all the information you need:

Practical Motor Cruising by Dag Pike tells you everything about boat handling and preparing yourself and your boat for sea, from one of the acknowledged experts in the field.

Fast Boats in Rough Seas by the same author takes you to a more advanced level.

Marine Inboard Engines by Loris Goring is the most up-to-date and comprehensive manual on this subject, aimed at those who want to know more about this most vital of components on a motorboat.

These will soon be joined by *Fast Boat Navigation* and *The Outboard Motor Manual*.

And of course, every month *Motorboats Monthly* brings you the latest news, boat tests, product reviews and practical information for those who get afloat under power. See you on the water.

Boatbuilders by type
of craft

The following is a selection of manufacturers of different types of craft. In the case of UK boats the name of the builder is given, from whom you can obtain the name of your nearest dealer. In the case of foreign makes the name of the UK importer is given.

Inflatables

Achilles South Western Marine Factors Ltd, 43 Pottery Rd, Parkstone, Poole, Dorset BH14 3RE. *Tel:* 0202 745414.

Avon Avon Inflatables Ltd, Dafen, Llanelli, Dyfed SA14 8NA. *Tel:* 0554 759171.

Bombard Zodiac UK Ltd, 2 Edgemead Close, Round Spinney, Northampton NN3 4RG. *Tel:* 0604 481214.

Flatacraft Flatacraft Ltd, 1183 Melton Rd, Syston, Leicester LE7 8JT. *Tel:* 0533 608468.

GB B P Barrus Ltd, Launton Rd, Bicester, Oxfordshire OX6 0UR. *Tel:* 0869 253355.

Humber Humber Inflatables Ltd, 246 Wincolmlee, Hull HU2 0PZ. *Tel:* 0482 22610.

Lifeguard Lifeguard Equipment Ltd, Lon Parcwr, Ruthin, Clwyd LL15 1YU. *Tel:* 08242 4314.

Maestral ManRo Leisure Marketing, Unit 24G, Morelands Trading Estate, Bristol Rd, Gloucester GL1 5RZ. *Tel:* 0425 500797.

Metzeler Metzeler Inflatables, Unit 2B, Park End Works, Croughton, Brackley, Northamptonshire NN13 5UN. *Tel:* 0869 810890.

Narwhal Narwhal UK, 58 Chingford Mount Road, Chingford, London E4 9AA. *Tel:* 081 531 9491.

Zodiac Zodiac UK Ltd, 2 Edgemead Close, Round Spinney, Northampton NN3 4RG. *Tel:* 0604 48124.

Runabouts

Aquaviva Marlin International Ltd, Chartwood House, Breamore, Hampshire SP6 2EF. *Tel:* 0726 22472.

Bayliner Windermere Aquatic Ltd, Bowness, Cumbria. *Tel:* 09662 2121.

Bonwitco Kingsbridge, Devon TQ7 1DE. *Tel:* 0548 2453.

Boston whaler Dorset Yacht Co. Ltd, Lake Drive, Hamworthy, Poole, Dorset BH15 4DT. *Tel:* 0202 674532.

Broom Jack Broom Boats Ltd, Brundall Gardens, Norwich NR13 5RG. *Tel:* 0603 712136.

Concorde Concorde International Powerboats Ltd, Castle Pill, Milford Haven, Dyfed *Tel:* 064262 2787.

Cranchi George Gould Marine, Sides Tumble In, South Stoke, Goring-on-Thames, Reading RG8 0JS. *Tel:* 0491 873387.

Dell Quay Dory Dell Quay Marine, Lake Ave, Hamworthy, Poole, Dorset BH15 4NY. *Tel:* 0202 679517.

Fletcher Fletcher International Sportsboats Ltd, New Road, Burntwood, Staffordshire WS7 0AZ. *Tel:* 0534 62181.

Flipper Macclesfield Marina, Brook St, Macclesfield, Cheshire SK11 7AW. *Tel:* 0625 20042.

Nauticalia, Ferry Lane, Shepperton, Middlesex. *Tel:* 0932 244396.

Four Winns Outboard Marine UK Ltd, 8 Harrowden Rd, Brackmills, Northampton NN4 0PD. *Tel:* 0604 765131.

Orkney Orkney Boats, Ford Lane Ind Est, Yapton, Arundel, Sussex BN18 0DF. *Tel:* 0243 551456.

Picton Picton Boats Ltd, Tondu Road, Bridgend, Mid Glamorgan. *Tel:* 0656 50695.

Plancraft Plancraft Marine Ltd, 6 The Street, Wrecclesham, Farnham, Surrey GU10 4PR. *Tel:* 0252 727440.

Sea Ray Lewis Marine Ltd, 59 High Street, Wanstead, London. *Tel:* 081 989 2265.

MDL Boat Sales Ltd, Penton Hook Marina, Chertsey. *Tel:* 0932 862211.

Spirit Spirit Marine, 1a Cutters Close, Narborough, Leicestershire LE9 5FY. *Tel:* 0533 848350.

Wellcraft George Bell Marine, Heath End Road, Nuneaton, Warwickshire. *Tel:* 0203 347870.

River boats

Alphacraft Alphacraft, Riverside Estate, Brundall, Norwich NR13 5PS. *Tel:* 0603 713265.

Atlanta Fibreglass Construction Ltd, Junction St, Burnley, Lancashire, BB12 0NX. *Tel:* 0282 27018.

Beaves Beaves Marine Ltd, Woodrolfe Road, Tollesbury, Essex. *Tel:* 0621 869270.

Birchwood Birchwood Boat International Ltd, Common Road, Huthwaite, Sutton in Ashfield, Nottinghamshire NG17 2JU. *Tel:* 0623 515133.

Brinks Barnes Brinkcraft, Riverside Rd, Norfolk NR12 8UD. *Tel:* 06053 2625.

Broom C J Broom & Sons Ltd, Brundall, Norwich, Norfolk NR13 5PX. *Tel:* 0603 712334.

Carver Racecourse Yacht Basin (Windsor) Ltd, Maidenhead Road, Windsor, Berkshire SL4 5HT. *Tel:* 0753 851717.

Fairline Fairline Boats Plc, Oundle PE8 5PA. *Tel:* 0832 73661.

Flipper Nauticalia Boats, Ferry Works, Shepperton, Middlesex. *Tel:* 0932 254844.

Hardy Hardy Marine Ltd, Gaymers Way Ind Est, North Walsham, Norfolk NR28 0AN. *Tel:* 0692 402885.

Highbridge Venetian Marine (Nantwich) Ltd, Cholmondeston, Nantwich, Cheshire. *Tel:* 0270 73251.

Kempala Better Boating Co, Mill Green, Caversham, Reading, Berkshire RG4 8EX. *Tel:* 0734 479536.

Linssen Boat Showrooms of London, Shepperton Marina, Felix Lane, Shepperton, Middlesex TW17 8NJ. *Tel:* 0932 243722.

Mayland Mayland Marine, Steeple Rd, Lower Mayland, Essex CM3 6BE. *Tel:* 0621 740518.

Nimbus Offshore Powerboats Ltd, Lymington Yacht Haven, Kings Saltern Rd, Lymington, Hampshire. *Tel:* 0590 77955.

Pedro Pedro Boats UK, 49 Victoria Rd, Deal, Kent CT14 7AY. *Tel:* 0304 364950.

Princess Marine Projects Ltd, Newport St, Plymouth, Devon PL1 3QG. *Tel:* 0752 227771.

Sealine Sealine International Ltd, Whitehouse Rd, Kidderminster, Worcester. *Tel:* 0562 740900.

Shadow Shadow Cruisers, Shore Rd, Warsash, Hampshire SO3 6FR. *Tel:* 0489 885400.

Shetland Shetland Cruisers Ltd, Redgrave Common, Redgrave, Norfolk. *Tel:* 0379 898496.

Viking Viking Mouldings,
Unit 11, Ongar Rd, Dunmow,
Essex CM6 1EU. *Tel:* 0371
5214.

Wave Rider Wave Rider
Marine Sales Ltd, Unit 7
Inland Warehousing Estate,
Tolleshunt Major, Nr
Maldon, Essex CM9 8LZ. *Tel:*
0621 868807.

Weston Weston Boats,
Waldergraves, West Mersea,
Colchester, Essex CO5 8SE.
Tel: 0206 385320.

Wilderness Wilderness Boats,
The Wilderness, Stokes Row,
Corsham, Wiltshire. *Tel:*
0249 712231.

Canal boats

Colcraft Colcraft Engineering
Ltd, Southam Road, Long
Itchington, Rugby,
Warwickshire. *Tel:* 092 681
4081.

Kate Kate Boats, The
Boatyard, Nelson Lane,
Warwick, Warwickshire
CV34 5JB. *Tel:* 0926 492968.

Piper David Piper
(Boatbuilders) Red Bull
Basin, Church Lawton, Stoke
on Trent, ST7 3AJ. *Tel:* 0782
784754.

Rugby Rugby Boatbuilders,
Hillmorton Wharf, Crick
Road, Rugby, Warwickshire
CV21 4PW. *Tel:* 0788
544438.

Springer Springer
Engineering Ltd, Unit L,
Valley Way Ind Estate,
Valley Way, Market
Harborough, Leicestershire.
Tel: 0858 62982.

Stroudwater Stroudwater
Narrowboat Co, Engine
Lane, Stourport on Severn.
Tel: 02993 77222.

Sea-going cruisers

Advance Alliance Agencies
Ltd, Unit 14–15 Cougar
Quay, School Lane, Hamble,
Southampton SO3 9XX. *Tel:*
0703 455341.

Allington Allington Marina
Ltd, Allington, Maidstone,
Kent ME16 0NH. *Tel:* 0622
52057.

Angel Angel Marine Ltd, Glen
Eldon House, Brighton Road,
Medstead, Alton, Hampshire.
Tel: 0420 64067.

Aqua Bell Aqua Bell Ltd,
Waterside, Brundall, Norfolk
NR13 5PY. *Tel:* 0603
713013.

Aqua-Star Aqua-Star Ltd,
Ocean Yard, Bulwer Ave, St
Sampson, Guernsey, Channel
Islands. *Tel:* 0481 44550.

Aquaviva Marlin
International Ltd, Chartwood
House, Breamore,
Hampshire SP6 2EF. *Tel:*
0725 22472.

Barracuda Greenaway
Marine Ltd, Broad Hinton,

Swindon, Wiltshire SN4 9PA. *Tel:* 0793 731666/7.

Bayliner Windermere Aquatic Ltd, Bowness, Cumbria. *Tel:* 09662 2121

Beaux Bateaux Beaux Bateaux, Nene Valley Business Park, Oundle, Peterborough PE8 4HN. *Tel:* 0832 274199.

Birchwood Birchwood Boat International Ltd, Common Road, Huthwaite, Sutton in Ashfield, Nottinghamshire NG17 2JU. *Tel:* 0623 515133.

Boston Whaler Dorset Yacht Co. Ltd, Lake Drive, Hamworthy, Dorset BH15 4DT. *Tel:* 0202 674531.

Bounty Bounty Boats Ltd, Riverside Estate, Brundall, Norwich. *Tel:* 0603 712070.

Broom C J Broom & Sons Ltd, Brundall, Norfolk NR13 5PX. *Tel:* 0603 712334.

Carver Racecourse Yacht Basin (Windsor) Ltd, Maidenhead Rd, Windsor, Berkshire SL4 5HT. *Tel:* 0753 851717.

Channel Islands Ian R. Driver, Mead End Road, Sway, Lymington SO41 6EE. *Tel:* 0590 682320.

Chris Craft Outboard Marine UK Ltd, 8 Harrowden Rd, Brackmills, Northampton NN4 0PD. *Tel:* 0604 765131.

Coastworker Coastworker Boats, 144 Furzebrook Rd, Wareham, Dorset BH20 5AR. *Tel:* 09295 51406.

Colvic Colvic Craft Plc, Earls Colne Ind Estate, Colchester, Essex. *Tel:* 0787 223993.

Corvette Corvette Cruisers Ltd, Unit 5 Meadow Lane Trading Estate, Meadowlane, Nottingham NG2 3HQ. *Tel:* 0602 864472.

Cougar Cougar Holdings Ltd, School Lane, Hamble, Southampton SO3 5JD. *Tel:* 0703 453513.

Cox Cox Marine Ltd, The Shipyard, Brightlingsea, Essex CO7 0AR. *Tel:* 0206 302840.

Cranchi George Gould, Sides Tumble In, South Stoke, Goring-on-Thames, Reading RG8 0JS. *Tel:* 0491 873387.

Darragh Darragh Ltd, Newbliss, Co. Monaghan, Ireland. *Tel:* 047 54022.

Delvo Boats Delvo Boats, Chapel Yard, Mossley Road, Hetton, Tyne & Wear. *Tel:* 091 526 9212.

Donzi Outboard Marine (UK) Ltd, 8 Harrowden Rd, Brackmills, Northampton NN4 0PD. *Tel:* 0604 765131.

Doral Roger Clark (Marine) Ltd, St Johns, Narborough, Leicester. *Tel:* 0533 848884.

Draco Bob Spalding Ltd, The Suffolk Yacht Harbour, Levington, Ipswich. *Tel:* 0473 88674.

Salterns Marine Sales, Salterns Marine, Lilliput, Poole, Dorset. *Tel:* 0202 700700.

Dyna Craft Dyna Craft (UK) Sales Ltd, PO Box 125, High Street, Sevenoaks, Kent TN13 1HR. *Tel:* 0752 740624.

Ernecraft Ernecraft Ltd, Lisnaskea, Co. Fermanagh, N. Ireland. *Tel:* 03657 21555.

Fairline Fairline Boats Plc, Oundle, PE8 5PA. *Tel:* 0832 73661.

Falcon Falcon Sportsboats Ltd, Griffin Lane, Norwich NR7 0SL. *Tel:* 0603 35516.

Fletcher Fletcher International Sportsboats Ltd, New Road, Burntwood, Staffordshire WS7 0AZ. *Tel:* 06436 2181.

Flipper Nauticalia Boats, Ferry Works, Shepperton, Middlesex. *Tel:* 0932 254844.

Flyer Beneteau UK Ltd, PO Box 5, Hamble, Hampshire. *Tel:* 0703 454022.

Formula Abersoch Land & Sea, Abersoch, Gwynedd, N. Wales LL53 7AH. *Tel:* 0758 813434.

Four Winns Outboard Marine (UK) Ltd, 8 Harrowden Rd, Brackmills, Northampton. *Tel:* 0604 765131.

Grand Banks Grand Banks Marketing, Shepperton Marina, Felix Lane, Shepperton, Middlesex TW17 8NJ. *Tel:* 0932 243722.

Halmatic Halmatic Ltd, Brookside Rd, Havant, Hampshire PO9 1JR. *Tel:* 0705 486161.

Hardy Hardy Marine Ltd, Gaymers Way Ind Est, North Walsham, Norfolk NR28 0AN. *Tel:* 0692 402885.

Hatteras Shamrock Quay, William St, Southampton, Hampshire SO1 1QL. *Tel:* 0703 330264.

Hershine Newberry Maine Ltd, The Slipway, Port Solent, Portsmouth, Hampshire. *Tel:* 0705 201071.

Hi-star Orient Yachts (UK) Ltd, Marine House, The Quay, Lymington, Hampshire. *Tel:* 0590 676393.

Humber F Booker Marine, Fall Bank Ind Est, Dodworth, Barnsley, S. Yorkshire. *Tel:* 0226 288388.

Humphrey Chris Humphrey (Boatbuilders) Riverside, Teignmouth, Devon, *Tel:* 06267 2324.

Hunton Hunton Powerboats, Unit 2 Budds Lane Industrial Estate, Romsey, Hampshire SO51 0HA. *Tel:* 0794 524153.

Invader Invader Boats UK, 296 Bridge Rd, Swanwick. *Tel:* 0489 885615.

Joda Buckden Marina and Leisure Club, Mill Road, Buckden, Huntingdon, Cambridgeshire PE18 9RY. *Tel:* 0480 810355.

Johnson Pacific Motor Yachts, 10 Scotts Close, Golden Common, Winchester SO21 1US. *Tel:* 0962 712018.

Kempala Better Boating Co, Mill Green, Caversham, Reading RG4 8EX. *Tel:* 0734 479536.

Landguard Landguard Marine, Shotley Point Marina, Shotley Gate, Ipswich IP9 1QJ. *Tel:* 0473 34557.

Linssen Boat Showrooms of London, Shepperton Marina, Felix Lane, Shepperton, Middlesex TW17 8NJ. *Tel:* 0932 243722.

Lochin Lochin Marine (Rye) Ltd, Rock Channel, Rye, E. Sussex TN31 7HJ. *Tel:* 0797 223724.

Marlin Marlin Marine Ltd, Hill Barton Ind. Estate, Sidmouth Rd, Clyst St Mary, Devon EX5 1DR. *Tel:* 0395 33250.

Mastercraft Mastercraft Boat Co., Great North Rd, Knottingley, W. Yorkshire WF11 0BS. *Tel:* 0977 676165.

Maxum Windsor Marine Sales, Windsor Marina, Maidenhead Rd, Windsor, Berkshire SL4 5TZ. *Tel:* 0753 860303.

Mayland Mayland Marine, Steeple Rd, Lower Mayland, Essex CM3 6BE. *Tel:* 0621 740518.

Neptune Neptune, 26 Shamrock Way, Hythe Marina Village, Southampton, Hants SO4 6DY. *Tel:* 0703 207143.

Nimbus Offshore Powerboats Ltd, Lymington Yacht Haven, Kings Saltern Rd, Lymington, Hampshire. *Tel:* 0590 77955.

Ocean Alexander Ocean Alexander (UK) Ltd, Quay St, Lymington, Hants. *Tel:* 0590 72909.

Pedro Pedro Boats (UK) Ltd, 49 Victoria Rd, Deal, Kent CT14 7AY. *Tel:* 0304 364950.

Picton Picton Boats Ltd, Trews Field Estate, Tondu Rd, Bridgend, Mid Glamorgan. *Tel:* 0656 50695.

Plancraft Plancraft Marine, Dapdune Wharf, Guildford, Surrey GU1 4RP. *Tel:* 0483 505995.

President Pacific Motor Yachts, 10 Scotts Close, Golden Common, Winchester SO21 1US. *Tel:* 0962 712018.

Princess Marine Projects Ltd, Newport Street, Plymouth,

Devon PL1 3QG. *Tel:* 0752 227771.

Prout Prout Catamarans Ltd, The Point, Canvey Island, Essex SS8 7TL. *Tel:* 0268 697462.

Pursuit Ancasta Marine Ltd, Port Hamble, Satchell Lane, Hamble, Hampshire SO3 5QD. *Tel:* 0703 455411.

Quayline Leisurecruise Ltd, Quay House, Bridge Road, Swanwick. *Tel:* 0489 885615.

Reliance S O Marine Enterprises, Westons Point Boatyard, Turks Lane, Poole, Dorset. *Tel:* 0202 715579.

Revenger Revenger Boat Co., Foreward Buildings, 46 Windsor Road, Slough, Berkshire. *Tel:* 0753 25496.

Ring Ring Powercraft, Unit W, Riverside Industrial Estate, Littlehampton, W. Sussex BN17 5DF. *Tel:* 0903 731317.

Rinker Morgan & Sons, 32–47 Waterside, Brightlingsea, Essex. *Tel:* 0206 302003.

Riva Lewis Marine Ltd, 59–61 High St, Wanstead, London E11 2AE. *Tel:* 081 989 2265.

Royal Paul Hadley, 30 Westgate, Chichester, West Sussex, PO19 3EU. *Tel:* 0243 785031.

Scand Express Cruisers, Quay St, Lymington, Hampshire. *Tel:* 0590 79355.

Seacoral Court Yard, 44 Gloucester Ave, Regents Park, London NW1 8JD. *Tel:* 071 586 9771.

Sealine Sealine International Ltd, Whitehouse Rd, Kidderminster, Worcester. *Tel:* 0562 740900.

Sea Ray Lewis Marine Ltd, 59 High St, Wanstead, London. *Tel:* 081 989 2265.

Penton Hook Marina, Staines Rd, Chertsey, Surrey. *Tel:* 0932 562211.

Seaward Seaward Marine Ltd, Hure Mare Ind. Estate, Vale, Guernsey, Channel Islands. *Tel:* 0481 45353.

Shadow Shadow Cruisers, Shore Rd, Warsash, Hampshire SO3 6FR. *Tel:* 0489 885400.

Shetland Shetland Cruisers Ltd, Redgrave Common, Redgrave, Norfolk. *Tel:* 0379 898496.

Slickcraft C2 International Marine Ltd, Forest Rd, Pyrford, Woking, Surrey. *Tel:* 09323 43916.

Sovereign Sovereign International, Yareside Gardens, Brundall, Norfolk.

Spirit Spirit Powerboats Ltd, 1a Cutters Close, Narborough, Leicester LE9 5FY. *Tel:* 0533 848350.

De Stevens Harleyford Marine Ltd, Shepperton Marina, Felix Lane,

Shepperton, Middlesex. *Tel:* 0932 243722.

Succes Notus International (CI) Ltd, Suitel Tower Bridge House, Le Bordage, St Peter Port, Guernsey, Channel Islands. *Tel:* 0481 713099.

Sunbird Outboard Marine UK Ltd, 8 Harrowden Road, Brackmills, Northampton NN4 0PD. *Tel:* 0604 765131.

Suncruiser Suncruiser Boats, Telford Rd, Gose Lane Ind. Estate, Clacton on Sea CO15 4LP. *Tel:* 0255 476496.

Sunray Focus Marine, 15 Shamrock Way, Hythe Marina Village, Southampton SO4 6DY. *Tel:* 0703 207101.

Sunrunner Gibbs Marine Sales, Russell Rd, Shepperton, Middlesex. *Tel:* 0932 242977.

Sunseeker Sunseeker International Powerboats Ltd, 27/31 West Quay Road, Poole, Dorset BH15 1HX. *Tel:* 0202 675071.

Swift Swift Boats Ltd, 9 The Square, Wickham, Hampshire PO1 5JQ. *Tel:* 0329 834403.

Teka Gibbs Marine Sales, Russell Road, Shepperton, Middlesex. *Tel:* 0932 242977.

Tiara Ancasta Marine Ltd, Port Hamble, Satchell Lane, Hamble, Hampshire SO3 5QD. *Tel:* 0703 455411.

Trader Tarquin Boat Co. Ltd, Tarquin House, Picket Hill, Ringwood, Hampshire BH24 3HH. *Tel:* 04254 5481.

Tremlett Tremlett Boat Sales Ltd, Topsham, Devon EX3 0PD. *Tel:* 039287 3680.

Viking Viking Mouldings, Unit 11, Ongar Rd, Dunmow, Essex CM6 1EU. *Tel:* 0371 5214.

Wave Rider Wave Rider Marine Sales Ltd, Unit 7, Inland Warehousing Estate, Tolleshunt Major, Nr. Maldon, Essex CM9 8LZ. *Tel:* 0621 868807.

Wellcraft George Bell Marine, Heath End Road, Nuneaton, Warwickshire. *Tel:* 0203 347870.

Western Yachts Western Yachts, Penpol Boatyard, Feock, Truro, Cornwall. *Tel:* 0872 862478.

Weston Weston Boats, Waldergraves, West Mersea, Colchester, Essex CO5 8SE. *Tel:* 0206 385320.

Whitewater Whitewater International, Hamble Point Marina, Hamble, Southampton. *Tel:* 0703 453071.

Windy Express Cruisers, Quay Street, Lymington, Hampshire. *Tel:* 0590 79355.

Useful addresses

British Marine Industries Federation   Boating Industry House, Vale Road, Weybridge, Surrey KT13 9NS. *Tel:* 0932 854511.

British Hire Cruiser Federation
Canals and Rivers
Association of Pleasure Craft Operators, 35a High St, Newport, Salop TF10 8JW. *Tel:* 0952 813572.
Thames
29 Bishop Ave, Bromley, Kent BR1 3ET. *Tel:* 081 464 8055.

British Waterways   Melbury House, Melbury Toe, London NW1 6JX. *Tel:* 071 262 671.

HM Customs & Excise   New Kings Beam House, 22 Upper Ground, London SE1 9PJ. *Tel:* 071 620 1313.

Inland Waterways Association   114 Regents Park Road, London NW1 8UQ. *Tel:* 071 586 1510.

National Rivers Authority   30–34 Albert Embankment, London SE1 7TL. *Tel:* 071 820 0101.

Royal National Lifeboat Institution   West Quay Rd, Poole, Dorset BH15 1HZ. *Tel:* 0202 671133.

Royal Yachting Association   RYA House, Romsey Road, Eastleigh, Hampshire SO5 4YA. *Tel:* 0703 629962.

Yacht Brokers, Designers & Surveyors Association   Wheel House, Petersfield Road, Whitehill, Bordon, Hampshire GU35 9BU. *Tel:* 04203 3862.

Major UK boat shows and events

The dates for these are only approximate, as they alter from year to year. For more accurate information refer to boating magazines, or contact the BMIF Boatline service on 0932 845890.

January	London International Boat Show
February	Birmingham Boat Show
	Glasgow Boat Show
April	Beaulieu Boat Jumble, Hampshire
	Bristol Boat Show
May	East Coast Boat Show, Ipswich
August	Inland Waterways National Rally (different locations each year)
September	Southampton International Boat Show

Get Afloat events are organised throughout the year by the British Marine Industries Federation (BMIF). Contact them on the Boatline number above for dates and places. See also pages 112 and 113.

———— Appendix 4 ————
Conversion table of principal dimensions

1 inch = 2.54 centimetres   1cm = 0.39in

1 foot = 0.305 metre   1m = 3.28ft

1 mile = 1.61 kilometres   1km = 0.62 mile

1 nautical mile = 6,060ft/1.1515 statute miles

1 pound = 0.45 kilogram   1kg = 2.205lb

1 ton = 2,240 pounds

1 tonne (metric ton) = 1,000 kilograms/1.016 tons

1 horsepower = 0.746 kilowatts   1kW = 1.34hp

1 pint = 0.57 litre   1 litre = 1.7 pints

1 gallon (Imperial) = 4.54 litres

1 Imperial gallon = 1.2 US gallons

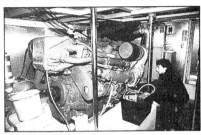

Volvo Penta
the boatbuilders choice

From the latest Princess and Fairline luxury cruisers at 60 feet and more to the new Sovereign inland waterways craft at under 30 feet – and pretty well every other leading motorboat name – you can expect the builder's power and performance preference to be Volvo Penta.

The largest supplier of marine inboard and inboard/outdrive engines to Britain's leisure boat builders, Volvo Penta has a purpose-designed package to power everything from a weekend runabout to a canal narrowboat to an ocean-going motor yacht. Right up more than 600hp from a single die: engine and 60 mph from a pet installation.

Volvo Penta, part of the internation Volvo Group, has been building mari engines for more than 80 years. Th have been years of technologi innovation.

A little over 30 years ago leisu boating was revolutionised by the arri of Volvo Penta's Aquamatic, whi brought together the best of t traditional propulsion principles: the board engine's protect environment and external drive's super manoeuvrability. Cop many times since never bettered.

Work on further rais the efficiencies of co bined engines and tra missions continued abated and culminat in another major bre through – Duoprop

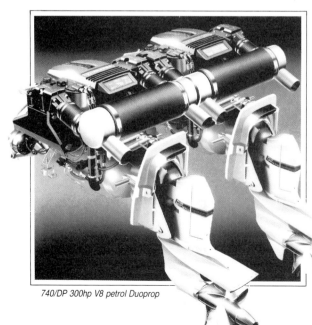

740/DP 300hp V8 petrol Duoprop

The Duoprop solution of two contra-rotating propellers located one behind the other on the same axle has been proven to increase acceleration by as much as 30%, reduce fuel consumption by around 10%, improve pulling power by at least 10% and add noticeably to top speed. Added to the performance are enhanced manoeuvrability and comfort of ride. Duoprop is available for both diesel and petrol engines.

MD 22 59hp 4 cylinder diesel

cylinder 10 valve units and powerful V6s and V8s. A total of more than 50 marine engine models from which to choose.

Behind it all is a nationwide sales and service dealer network, the largest of its kind in the UK and part of an international organisation operating in more than 130 countries. Wherever you are likely to go boating.

There is all the advice, assistance and care that the newcomer to motorboating night need, from the biggest name in marine engines technology.

TAMD 71B 380hp 6 cylinder turbo diesel

Today's diesel engine programme at Volvo Penta encompasses units from compact one, two and three cylinder versions to the bigger four and six cylinder models, many available with turbocharging – which Volvo Penta helped pioneer – and aftercooling. The petrol engines range is based on four

VOLVO PENTA
Power
PERFORMANCE

British Marine INDUSTRIES FEDERATION

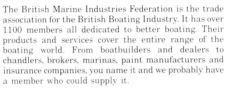

The British Marine Industries Federation is the trade association for the British Boating Industry. It has over 1100 members all dedicated to better boating. Their products and services cover the entire range of the boating world. From boatbuilders and dealers to chandlers, brokers, marinas, paint manufacturers and insurance companies, you name it and we probably have a member who could supply it.

So how do you find out more about boating? Simple! *Call BOATLINE. 0932 845890.*

Boatline

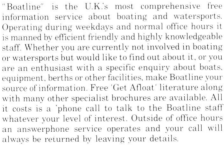

"Boatline" is the U.K.'s most comprehensive free information service about boating and watersports. Operating during weekdays and normal office hours it is manned by efficient friendly and highly knowledgeable staff. Whether you are currently not involved in boating or watersports but would like to find out about it, or you are an enthusiast with a specific enquiry about boats, equipment, berths or other facilities, make Boatline your source of information. Free 'Get Afloat' literature along with many other specialist brochures are available. All it costs is a 'phone call to the Boatline staff whatever your level of interest. Outside of office hours an answerphone service operates and your call will always be returned by leaving your details.

Remember Boatline. Your first 'Port of Call' for boating information.

TRY A BOAT

The Boatline staff can also provide you with details of the free **Try A Boat** events held around the U.K. every year. Approximately 15 events take place each year at different locations from April through to September. A wide range of boats are available and crewed by qualified instructors. A bouyancy aid is provided and wet weather gear if necessary.

There is no obligation at all just an ideal opportunity to 'get afloat' and have a highly enjoyable time!

Call *BOATLINE* for the date and venue of the nearest event to you.